Recipe *for* Disaster

Compiled by
Aisling Brennan
Arlene North

Photographs by the Irish Orthopaedic Team February 2010
www.iohf.ie

Printed by R&S Printers Ltd. Monaghan

Published by
© Irish Institute of Trauma & Orthopaedic Surgery
(IITOS) 2011

ISBN 978-0-9567911

Partners in Health

For your outstanding and selfless contributions to Operation Smile.
Your dedication and commitment have ensured the continuing success of our volunteer
medical services to provide new lives for the children of Haiti.
Our deep and sincere appreciation for helping us create miracles for these children.

International Mission
Hinche, Haiti
December 8-14,2008

FOREWORD - IITOS

On 12th January 2010 a devastating earthquake hit Haiti. In its aftermath a group of Irish Orthopaedic surgeons from the Irish Institute of Trauma & Orthopaedic Surgery (IITOS) visited the country to see if there was scope for the Irish orthopaedic community to help in the relief efforts. The amount and severity of injuries sustained in the earthquake was shocking. While on our visit we were fortunate to meet with Dr. Louise Ivers, an Irish doctor who works in Haiti. Dr. Ivers is the medical director in Haiti for a Boston based charity called Partners in Health that runs 10 hospitals in the country.

Unlike most hospitals in the area these hospitals provide care free of charge to the poor. We visited a hospital in Cange (North of Port Au Prince) where we were able to operate on patients with injuries sustained in the earthquake. The hospital in Cange ordinarily provides mainly obstetric and paediatric services with some general surgery. It did not have the expertise or equipment to deal with the range of injuries from the earthquake. Partners in Health were coordinating teams of trauma and orthopaedic surgeons from mainly the USA to deal with these patients. As a result of our meeting and experience we were able to offer to Dr. Ivers the services of teams from Ireland to assist with their efforts.

Since February 2010 we have sent numerous teams over to Cange to provide rehabilitation services to survivors of the earthquake. The teams have consisted of Plastic and Orthopaedic Surgeons, Anaesthetists, Nursing and Physiotherapy staff and logistical personnel. Rehabilitation services in the form of surgery, advanced nursing care, physiotherapy and limb fitting are essential to help people resume any sort of normal life.

Our relationship with Partners in Health is continuing. Plans are in place to build a hospital, including a purpose-built orthopaedic facility for Haitian patients. We expect to establish an orthopaedic surgical training programme which we will run in conjunction with the Haitian department of Health and Partners in Health. This will involve regular visits to Haiti, approximately 8 -10 times per year.

All our efforts to date have been possible due to donations, fundraising projects and the willingness of Irish health care professionals to provide their time as volunteers. This project does not have any paid staff and our administrative costs to date are zero. Any money raised from the sale of this book "Recipe for Disaster" will be used directly to support our ongoing efforts.

Mr. David Moore
President, IITOS

Mr. Keith Synnott
Director of Training, IITOS

Foreword

On the 13th February we travelled to Cange, Haiti to help in the rehabilitation of patients who suffered injuries in the earthquake on 12th January 2010. Despite our experience in Ireland of treating Orthopaedic injuries we were overwhelmed at the volume and complexity of injuries sustained by some of the patients that faced us on our arrival in Cange. Not only had these people significant physical injuries they also had suffered extreme personal loss from the Earthquake. It was impossible not to be affected by the poverty. These people have lost what little they had before the earthquake. They have lost family, homes and possessions and for many they have lost their "papers"; birth certificates, passports etc. They are a people without identity.

The on site church was converted to a ward to help cope with the influx of casualties. Many slept on air mattresses, some on unfolded chairs with family sleeping on the tiled floor beside them or on the concrete paths surrounding the hospital. No complaints were heard, just anxious questions about bone and wound healing underpinned with concern for loss of limb. There was no place for inhibitions or struggle for private rooms! It was common practice for all concerned family members to come and observe treatment and even to offer help. The sense of community and helpfulness that these people had for each other was most humbling and perhaps could teach us a lesson or two.

They are a special group of people to work with and any advice, treatment, equipment given to patients was most gratefully received. One little girl was heard singing "God is so good, God is so good, He is so good to me" following a treatment session with one of our team. Singing became part of treatment sessions and was often used to distract and encourage patients. In one ward we taught some of the patients 'Ireland's call'. "Ireland, Ireland, together standing tall, shoulder to shoulder we will answer Ireland's call". It is up to us as a first world nation to answer Haiti's call. We will never forget the people, sights, smells and sounds of Haiti. More importantly let us not forget their suffering.

The idea of putting this recipe book together was born in Haiti as we enjoyed the local food. We wanted to highlight the diversity between European Cuisine and Haitian Cuisine and at the same time share our experience with you. We hope you enjoy the book that is made up of recipes from our team who travelled to Haiti, well-known Irish personalities and a selection of Haitian recipes. We are most grateful to all those who contributed. Not only is this a recipe book. Through "Recipe for Disaster" we hope to take you through the journey of the work that has been carried out by the IITOS in Haiti – the joy and hope of the Haitian people is evident throughout the photographic display. Enjoy.......

Aisling Brennan
Chartered Physiotherapist

Arlene North
Clinical Nurse Specialist

A Personal Message

HAITIAN FOOD

Haitian cuisine is kréyol cuisine, a mixture of French, African, Spanish and indigenous cooking methods, ingredients and dishes. Rice and beans (dire ak pwa) are a staple. Vegetable and meat stews are popular too. Goat, beef, chicken and fish are complemented with plantains, cabbage, tomatoes and peppers. Fiery Scotch bonnet peppers lend their punch to many dishes, and to pikliz, a popular pickled vegetable condiment.

Haitian Recipes

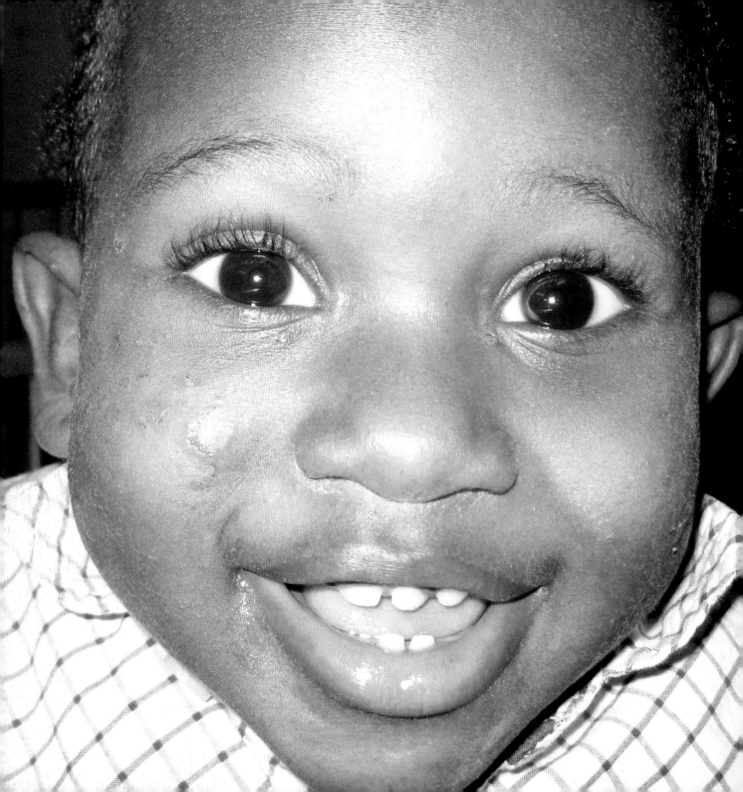

Haitian Soup (Boillion)

Ingredients

1 Malanga (Potato)
1 green pepper, sliced
3 carrots
2 onions sliced
1 tbsp thyme
1 tbsp parsley
¼ cup scallions
3 tbsp tomato paste
Salt, black pepper and hot pepper to taste.

Method

Clean meat with hot water and lemon.
Add seasoning, salt and set aside for 2 hours in a bowl.
Combine meat and spinach in a stockpot with 2 quarts of water and cook until meat is tender.
Add remaining ingredients and cook for an additional 20 minutes or until potatoes are cooked.

Recipe for Disaster
ALL PROCEEDS IN AID OF IRISH ORTHOPAEDIC HAITI FUND

Boeuf à l'Haïtienne

(Haitian beef with tomatoes and peppers) This simple, flavourful dish is characteristic of the Haitian love of tasty meat and vegetable dishes. Boeuf à l'haïtienne tastes even better if served the next day.

Ingredients (Serves 4-6)

1 pound Beef shoulder or chuck roast, cubed
2 tsp Salt
Water to cover
¼ cup Oil
1 Onion, thinly sliced
2 Red or green peppers, chopped
2 – 4 cloves Garlic, minced
1 - 4 Hot chilli pepper, minced
2 cups Tomatoes, seeded and chopped
1 tbsp Red wine vinegar
Salt and pepper to taste

Method

Place the beef and salt in a large pot and add enough water just to cover the meat. Bring to a boil over high heat, then reduce heat to low and simmer, uncovered, until the beef is tender and the water is almost completely evaporated, 45 minutes to an hour.
While the beef is simmering, heat the oil in a skillet over medium flame. Add the onion, peppers, garlic and chilli peppers and sauté until the onions and peppers are wilted.
Add the tomatoes, vinegar, salt and pepper. Reduce heat to low and simmer until almost all liquid is evaporated, 20-25 minutes.
Stir the beef into the onions and peppers and simmer for another 20-30 minutes, adding a little water if necessary. Adjust seasoning and serve with rice.

Chicken in Sauce

Ingredients

1 medium sized chicken
1 large onion sliced in rounds
1 large pepper (mild or hot depending on your taste)
Several cloves of garlic, smashed or minced
1- 4 cups of tomato sauce
3 tbsp sugar
Generous pinch of salt
Lime or lemon

Method

Wash chicken well and cut into pieces. Rub each piece with the lemon or lime and sprinkle with salt.
Heat oil in a heavy pan (cast iron is best, as the pan will then be placed in the oven)
Meanwhile, preheat the oven to 375° F and fry the chicken pieces in hot oil.
While the chicken is frying combine the garlic, sugar, tomato sauce and salt in a bowl and mix well.
After a few minutes add the onion rounds and pepper rounds to the pan, stir well.
Within a few minutes the chicken should be well browned. Remove from heat, drain excess oil and add the tomato mixture and stir well.
Place the entire pan in the oven and bake uncovered for 20 minutes or until the chicken is cooked completely.
Transfer cooked chicken to a platter and garnish with rounds of raw onion and a pile of picklese.

This dish goes well with diri blan (plain white rice).

Recipe for Disaster

All Proceeds in Aid of Irish Orthopaedic Haiti Fund

Rice Red Beans (Diri et Pois Coles)

Ingredients

2 cups of long grain rice
1 cup of kidney beans
1 finely chopped onion
1 chopped hot green pepper
¼ cup salt pork or bacon cut into small cubes
1 tbsp of butter
2 chopped gloves of garlic
2 tbsp of vegetable oil
Salt and pepper to taste

Method

Cook the beans in 4 cups of water for 2 hours or until tender.
Drain the beans but keep the water which will be used to cook the rice.
Fry salt pork or bacon until crisp (use oil if needed).
Add the onion, garlic and green pepper.
Add the beans along with salt and pepper to taste.
Add water used to cook the beans and bring to the boil.
Add the rice and cook for 20-25 minutes.

Meatballs (Boulette)

Ingredients

4 slices of bread
½ cup flour
½ cup grated parmesan cheese
1 cup milk
1lb freshly smoked ham or bacon minced
2 garlic gloves, minced
1 tbsp tomato paste
1 tbsp of oil

Method

Salt, black pepper and hot pepper to taste.
Put all ingredients except the oil in a large pan and marinade
for 4 hours.
Transfer meat mixture to medium saucepan or pressure cooker and add water to
cover.
Heat to boiling and reduce heat, simmer covered until meat
is very tender.
Remove and fry meat in a large pan until crisp and golden brown.

Recipe for Disaster
ALL PROCEEDS IN AID OF IRISH ORTHOPAEDIC HAITI FUND

Pikliz (vegetable dish)

Every Haitian home has a jar of pikliz on hand. Cabbage, carrots, chiles and other vegetables are soaked in vinegar to make a relish similar to American chow-chow or Italian giardiniera. The crunchy salad is served as a side dish at Haitian meals. Flavored vinegar from pikliz is often used in marinades or to give dishes a spicy-sour punch.

Ingredients

½ head Cabbage, shredded
2 Carrots, peeled and chopped into small pieces or grated
1 Onion, thinly sliced
2 - 6 Scotch bonnet peppers
4 - 6 Garlic cloves
2 tsp Salt
8 -10 Peppercorns
3 cups White or cane vinegar

Method

Add all of the ingredients to a large bowl and toss well to mix. Place all of the vegetables into a clean 2-quart glass jar. Pour in enough vinegar to cover the vegetables, pressing them down to remove any air bubbles.
Store the pikliz in the refrigerator for at least 24 hours before serving. It will keep in the refrigerator for a month or two.

Griots (Haitian Grillots -- fried, glazed pork)

This rich, flavourful dish is one of Haiti's most popular, invariably served at parties and family gatherings. Cubes of pork are soaked in a sour orange marinade and then slow-roasted until tender. The tender morsels are then given a finally fry in oil until delectably caramelized. This recipe uses a mixture of orange and lime juice in place of the hard-to-find sour orange juice. Also spelled grillots, griyo, griyot or griot.

Ingredients (Serves 6 to 8)

4 pounds Pork shoulder, cubed
1 Onion, thinly sliced
1 Green or red bell pepper, thinly sliced
1-2 Scotch bonnet peppers, chopped (optional)
2 - 3 Shallots/ 4-5 Scallions thinly sliced
3 - 4 cloves Garlic, chopped
2 tsp Thyme
2 tsp Salt
1 tsp Pepper
2 Oranges
3 Limes
1/4 cup Oil

Method

Add the pork and all the other ingredients except the oil to a large, non-reactive bowl and mix together well. Refrigerate for 4 to 24 hours to let the meat soak up the marinade.

Heat oven to 375°F. Place the pork and its marinade into a large roasting pan and cover tightly with a lid or aluminum foil. Place in the oven and roast for 1 1/2 to 2 hours, or until the pork is tender.

Remove the roasting pan from the oven. Remove any extra liquid in the pan, putting it into a saucepan, and set aside. Add the oil to the pan and stir it into the meat. Return the roasting pan to the oven and let the pork cook for 20 to 30 minutes more, stirring occasionally. Any liquid will evaporate away and the meat will begin to fry in the oil and brown.

While the meat is frying in the oven, place the saucepan with the reserved liquid on the top of the stove and boil it down until it is well reduced and thickens. Remove the roasting pan from the oven and mix the reduced sauce into the browned pork. Serve hot with with sos ti-malis, banan peze and a side of pikliz.

Variations Use sour orange juice if you can find it. Or substitute pikliz vinegar for some of the orange and lime juice if you like. Griots can also be made on the stovetop. Use a large Dutch oven with a tight-fitting lid.

Recipe for Disaster

ALL PROCEEDS IN AID OF IRISH ORTHOPAEDIC HAITI FUND

Diri Ole (Rice pudding)

Arroz con leche (rice with milk) is one of the most popular desserts in the Latin world. This simple sweet conjures up memories of home and is supreme comfort food.

Ingredients (Serves 4 to 6)

4 cups Milk
½ cup Short-grain rice
1 Cinnamon stick
2 strips Orange or lemon peel (optional)
Pinch Salt
¼ cup Raisins
½ cup Sugar
2 tbsp Butter
1 tsp Vanilla

Method

Place the milk, rice, cinnamon stick, orange or lemon peel and salt in a medium saucepan and bring to a boil over medium heat. Immediately reduce heat to very low and simmer, stirring often and scraping bottom, for about 45 minutes.
Add the raisins and sugar and simmer for another 15 minutes. Stir often to keep from sticking to the bottom of the pot.
Remove from heat and stir in the butter and vanilla. Adjust sugar to taste and serve hot or cold, sprinkling the top with some ground cinnamon.

Fried Bananas (Beyen)

Ingredients

3 very ripe bananas
1 tablespoon flour
½ tablespoon cinnamon powder
½ tablespoon vanilla extract
1 tablespoon sugar
1/8 tablespoon baking soda
Sugar for topping (optional)

Method

Mix bananas, flour, sugar, vanilla and cinnamon in medium size
bowl to make batter
Place spoonful of batter in very hot oil and fry until golden brown
Sprinkle with sugar

Starter Recipes

Recipe for Disaster

ALL PROCEEDS IN AID OF IRISH ORTHOPAEDIC HAITI FUND

Prawn Cocktail

Ingredients

1 ripe avocado
1 lemon
Approx 250g of cooked small peeled prawns
Lemon wedges, to garnish
For the Marie Rose Sauce:
Approx 200g fresh mayonnaise
2-3 tbsp tomato ketchup
Pinch cayenne pepper
Dash Tabasco, to taste
Dash Worcestershire sauce, to taste
Splash of brandy, to taste
Pinch of Paprika to garnish
½ iceberg lettuce

Method

Cut the avocado in half, remove the stone and carefully score each half using a small knife to create a criss-cross pattern. Squeeze each half generously with lemon juice to prevent it from dis-colouring.
To make the Marie Rose sauce mix the mayonnaise, ketchup, cayenne pepper, and a squeeze of lemon juice together in a large bowl. Season to taste with Tabasco, Worcestershire sauce, and a splash of brandy.
Stir to combine.
Place a spoonful of Marie Rose sauce into the bottom of 4 serving glasses. Shred the lettuce and divide equally among the glasses.
Scrape out the flesh from the avocado using a spoon and scatter over the lettuce. Spoon another layer of sauce on top.
Arrange the prawns on top and finish with a final spoonful of sauce. Sprinkle with a touch of cayenne pepper and paprika and garnish with a lemon wedge in each glass to serve.

Paul O'Connell Irish and Munster Rugby Star

Angel Hair Pasta with Killary Bay Prawns

Ingredients

150g angel hair pasta
3 tbsp olive oil
1 clove garlic- crushed
2 shallots - diced
50g tomatoes – chopped
2 tsp tomato purée
300ml double cream
8 prawn tail – raw, shells on
salt and black pepper to season
4 basil leaves
25 Parmesan – grated

Method

Remove prawn tails from shells and set aside
Cook pasta in boiling, salted water for 6 minutes. Drain, refresh in cold water and drain again.
Heat some oil in a pan, add garlic, prawn shells and shallots and cook for 2 –3 minutes.
Add tomato purée and simmer for 1 minute, add cream and reduce by a third.
Pass the sauce through a fine sieve and season. Heat remaining oil in a pan, add the prawns and cook for 2 minutes.
Mix in the pasta, diced tomatoes, basil leaves and sauce.
Season with salt and black pepper.
Serve with grated Parmesan.

While I use Killary Bay prawns any plump prawns will do. Make sure frozen prawns are well thawed before cooking. The delicacy of the fine pasta means that the sauce is not overpowered and the sweet flavour of the prawns comes through perfectly.

Tim O'Sullivan
Head Chef at Renvyle House Hotel Connemara, Co. Galway

Recipe for Disaster

ALL PROCEEDS IN AID OF IRISH ORTHOPAEDIC HAITI FUND

Vegetable Soup

Ingredients
Stock
The making of stock is very simple and involves placing the carcase of a chicken into a large pot of cold water adding a few onions (including the skins for colour and flavour), carrots and celery. I would also include 6 or 7 black pepper corns and 1 Knorr beef cube (the jelly one). I would also add some parts of a leek including the green end bit if you have any. This should simmer for 1½ to 2 hours.

Method
First thing is to sweat some vegetables which would normally include 2 or 3 carrots (skin can be left on), 2 large onions, 2 sticks of celery, 1 leek and 2 potatoes all chopped into smallish pieces. I would also add 2 or 3 fresh bay leaves and these should sweat for at least 10 minutes.
Then add approx. 4 large fresh tomatoes and continue to sweat for another few minutes. Season with salt and pepper (not too much salt needed because of the Knorr stock).
Add the stock and also add another Knorr beef cube and simmer for 30-40 mins.
Remove bay leaves and blitz.

My brother in law Pat Weafer, a great architect and a talented cook, taught me how to make this delicious Vegetable Soup. It's the best soup I have tasted especially on these cold winter days. This is a meal in itself and delicious with brown bread.

Martin Bolger Plaster Nurse (Haiti February 2010)

Tuna Fish Cakes

Ingredients

Vegetable oil for frying
1 finely chopped onion
A few chopped chives
500g ready-made or leftover mashed potato
2 200g jars or cans of tuna steak in spring water or drained from Brine
2 crushed matzo crackers
4 tbsp mayonnaise
4 tbsp tartare sauce
1 lemon

Method

Heat a little oil in a frying pan and fry a finely chopped onion
until softened.
Put into a large bowl and stir in a few chopped chives, mashed
potato and drained jars or cans of tuna steak. Season well.
Shape into 8 patties and press firmly into crushed matzo crackers until
well-coated.
Shallow-fry on both sides until golden, then drain on kitchen paper.
Mix mayonnaise, tartare sauce and a few more chopped chives. Serve
alongside the fish cakes with lemon wedges to squeeze over.

Rob Kearney Irish and Leinster Rugby Star

Recipe for Disaster
ALL PROCEEDS IN AID OF IRISH ORTHOPAEDIC HAITI FUND

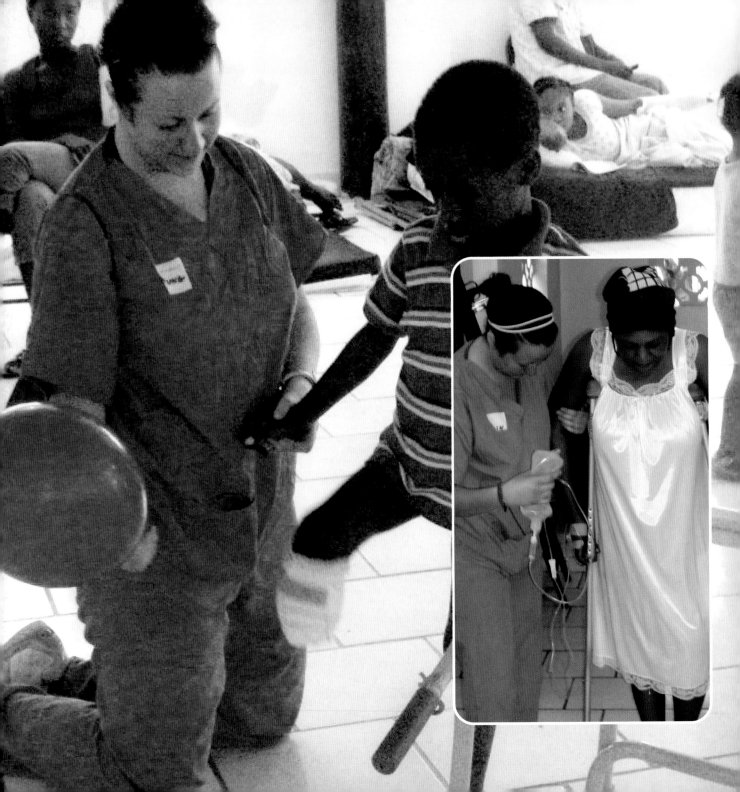

Asparagus and Parma Ham

Ingredients

12 spears of asparagus
12 slices of parma ham
Cream cheese (I use low fat Philadelphia cheese)
30g butter
Rocket leaves
Balsamic vinegar

Method

Set the oven to 180°C/gas 4.
Spread a layer of cream cheese on each slice of Parma Ham
Wrap the Parma Ham around the asparagus spears and lay each one
on a baking tray, brushing them lightly with butter to ensure they do
not stick.
Cook for 3-4 minutes until the asparagus is nicely roasted and the
ham is crispy.
Serve of a bed of rocket with a drizzle of balsamic vinegar.

*I like this recipe because it is easy to prepare, tastes yummy and people
always think you've put a lot of effort into its preparation. It's great as a starter or
as finger food with drinks before dinner. Enjoy!*

Aisling Brennan, Chartered Physiotherapist (Haiti February 2010)

Recipe *for* Disaster

ALL PROCEEDS IN AID OF IRISH ORTHOPAEDIC HAITI FUND

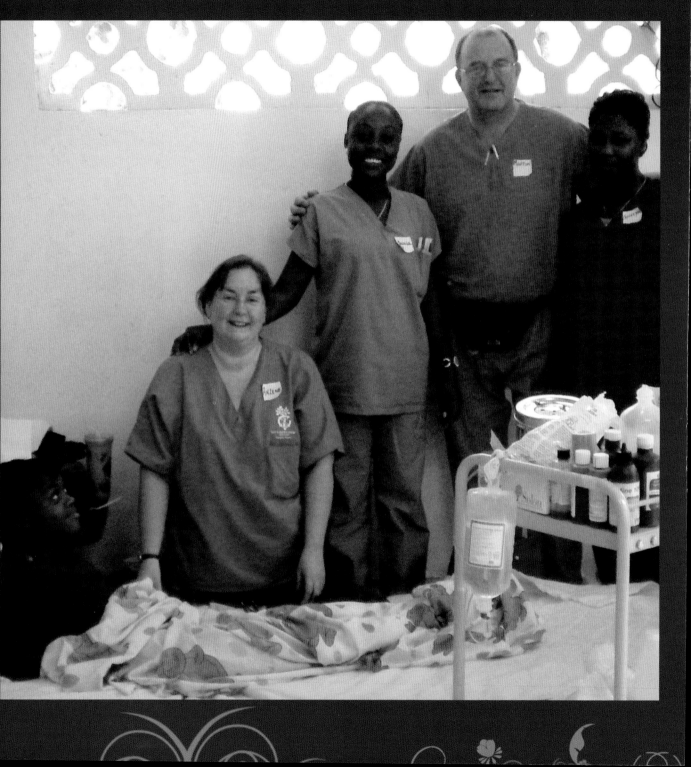

Courgette and Corn Chowder

Ingredients

500g/ 1lb potatoes
2 sticks of celery - finely chopped
2 pints chicken stock/ 1 litre
200g/7 oz sweet corn –
fresh or frozen
4 medium courgettes – sliced

125g/4oz mature cheddar
cheese- grated
80g/ 3 oz rocket leaves
1 large onion – chopped
250ml milk/1/4 pint
Salt and black pepper to season.

Method

Place the potato, onion, celery, courgette and stock in a large pan and bring to the
boil. Simmer, covered, until the vegetables are tender about 20 minutes. Leave to
cool slightly. Add rocket leaves. Blend until smooth.
Return to the heat, add the corn and cook for 5 minutes. Stir in the grated mature
Cheddar and milk, reheat gently. Do not boil. Season with salt and freshly ground
black pepper.
Serve with Melba toast or hot crusty rolls.

Arlene North Clinical Nurse Specialist, (Haiti February 2010)

Recipe for Disaster

ALL PROCEEDS IN AID OF IRISH ORTHOPAEDIC HAITI FUND

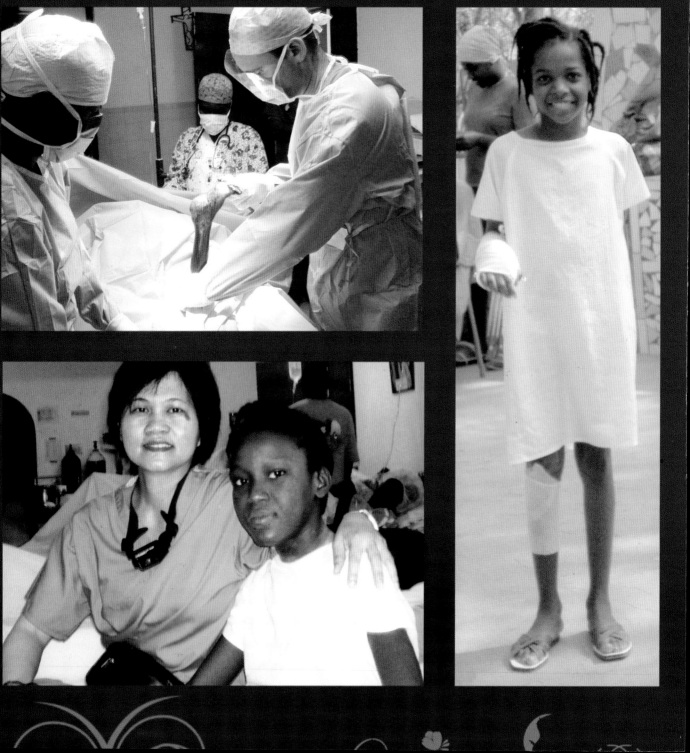

Hot and Sour Shrimp with Watercress and Walnuts

Ingredients (Serves 4)

1 lb Large uncooked shrimp, -peeled, deveined, -butterflied
4 tbsp Dry Sherry
1 tbsp Grated peeled fresh ginger
1/2 cup Chicken stock or canned -broth
2 tbsp Soy sauce
2 tbsp Catsup. [See note]
1 tbsp Cornstarch
1 tbsp Rice vinegar or white wine -vinegar
1 tbsp Sugar
1 tsp Oriental sesame oil
1/4 tsp Cayenne pepper
6 tbsp Peanut oil
2 tbsp Chopped walnuts
3 bunch Watercress, trimmed
2 medium Bell peppers, cut into -1-inch squares
2 Garlic cloves, minced
8 Green onions, cut -diagonally into -1-inch-long pieces

Method

A light marinade of Sherry and ginger flavours the shrimp, which are stir-fried with the bell peppers and green onions. Watercress makes a colorful bed for the shrimp.

Combine shrimp, 2 tablespoons Sherry and grated ginger in large bowl. Cover and refrigerate for 30 minutes. Mix remaining 2 tablespoons Sherry, chicken stock, soy sauce, catsup, cornstarch, rice vinegar, sugar, sesame oil and cayenne pepper in small bowl.

Heat 2 teaspoons peanut oil in wok or heavy large skillet over high heat. Add walnuts and stir-fry for 1 minute. Transfer walnuts to plate using slotted spoon. Add watercress to wok and stir-fry until just wilted, about 1 minute. Divide watercress among plates. Add 2 teaspoons peanut oil, bell peppers and garlic to wok and stir-fry for 1 minute. Add remaining 2 teaspoons peanut oil, shrimp mixture and onions and stir-fry for 1 minute. Stir stock mixture, add to wok and cook sauce until clear and thick, stirring frequently, 2 minutes.

Spoon sauce and shrimp over watercress. Sprinkle with walnuts and serve.

NOTE: You can use Jufran sauce rather than catsup. Jufran is a Philippino sauce that's looks and tastes much like catsup. It's made from bananas and other stuff, however and has a more complex and interesting taste. It comes in both mild and hot forms. The mild is not too hot++somewhat like a spicy catsup. The hot stuff is much hotter, although not intolerably so. If you use this, be prudent about how much cayenne you use, at least the first time until you can see how they balance out.

Josie Nacpil Theatre Nurse (Haiti February 2010)

Recipe for Disaster

ALL PROCEEDS IN AID OF IRISH ORTHOPAEDIC HAITI FUND

Hot and Spicy Mexican Chicken Skewers

Ingredients

3 tbsp olive oil
1 garlic clove, crushed
1 tsp ground cumin
1/2 tsp cayenne pepper
3 skinless chicken breasts, cut into bite-size pieces
1 small red pepper and 1 small green pepper, deseeded and cut into
bite-size pieces
1 small to medium onion, cut into 8 wedges
Small tub guacamole, to serve

Method

Put the oil, garlic and spices into a bowl and mix well. Add the
chicken to the marinade, mix and leave to marinate at room temperature
for 30 minutes.
Meanwhile, soak 8 bamboo or wooden skewers in cold water for the same time.
Thread the chicken, peppers and onion alternately onto the skewers.
Brush any remaining marinade onto the peppers and onion pieces. Put on
a cooking grate and cook directly over a medium heat source for 10-12
minutes, turning halfway.
Serve with guacamole.

Ronan O'Gara Irish and Munster Rugby Star

Springroll Of Duck and Spicy Stir-Fried Vegetables, with Pineapple and Spring Onion Salsa and Savoury Couscous

Ingredients

2 duck legs
4 tablespoons bean sprouts
half aubergine - finely sliced
30g green cabbage - shredded
25g ginger – grated
100ml chicken stock
4 sprigs fresh parsley
8 springroll pastry sheets
100g couscous
1 red chilli – diced

Pineapple and spring onion salsa

Mix together:
half fresh pineapple - diced
75g spring onion - diced
50g tomato – diced
8 chives – chopped
juice of 2 limes
2 tablespoons olive oil

Method

Heat oven to 200°C/440°F/ Gas mark 6 and roast duck legs for 1 hour
Remove skin from duck legs, discard and cut meat into strips
Stir fry vegetables and ginger; add duck meat and leave to cool
Soak couscous with the diced chilli in 100ml of chicken stock until all the stock is absorbed. Wrap duck and vegetables in pastry, sealing the edges with a little water and shape into rolls. Cook in hot oil for 3 – 4 minutes
Place a ring of couscous on the centre of the plate. Place two springrolls on top. Pour the salsa around the edge of the plate. Garnish with sprigs of parsley

The contrast of the duck with salsa, punctuated with sweet pineapple is perfect and makes a delicious light supper dish as well as a starter.

Tim O'Sullivan Head Chef at Renvyle House Hotel, Connemara, Co. Galway

STARTERS

Recipe for Disaster

ALL PROCEEDS IN AID OF IRISH ORTHOPAEDIC HAITI FUND

Parma Ham, Fig and Mozzarella Salad with Warm Pitta

Ingredients

Bag of wild rocket leaves
6 ripe figs
2 125g balls buffalo mozzarella
6 Parma ham slices
2 tbsp honey
1 tbsp lemon juice
1 tbsp lime juice
3 pitta breads

Method

Spill bag of wild rocket leaves onto a platter. Cut figs in half
and arrange on the leaves. Tear up balls of buffalo mozzarella and add
to the platter. Tear Parma ham slices into strips and arrange on the
platter.
Mix honey with lemon and lime juice and drizzle over the top.
Season with black pepper.
Pop a few pitta breads in the toaster and serve warm with the salad.

*I love this recipe, it is so quick and easy to do at home. Great after a long days
training when you need something quick and tasty at the same time.*

Luke Fitzgerald Irish and Leinster Rugby Star

Scallops and Chorizo Salad

Ingredients

3-4 scallops per person depending on size
(Fresh is best but frozen will do in a pinch)
2-3 chorizo (5mm discs) slices per person

Rocket salad leaves
Sweet baby plum tomatoes
Thinly sliced red onion or spring onions (to taste)

Salad Dressing

4 dsp of Good quality Extra Virgin Olive Oil
1/2 dsp of Balsamic vinegar
1 - 2 tsp of whole grain french mustard

Method

Heat a non-stick pan and add the slices of chorizo. The heat will provide you with sufficient oil to then add the scallops. Fry in the chorizo oil until lightly browned on each side. (1-2 minutes per side - depending on the scallop size and whether frozen or fresh)

Prepare salad and drizzle small amount of dressing before adding the scallops and chorizo.

Serve with crusty bread or foccacio and a glass of wine - pinot grigio is great with it!

This is a tasty and healthy recipe. The reason I chose it is because it's easy to prepare at short notice and it evokes the sunshine, of which we get all too little!

Ursula Gormally Co-ordinator of Irish Orthopaedic Haiti Fund and teams

Recipe for Disaster

ALL PROCEEDS IN AID OF IRISH ORTHOPAEDIC HAITI FUND

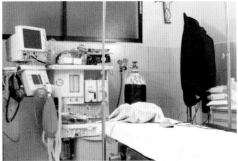

Spicy Pea Soup

Ingredients

1 tsp Olive oil
1 large onion, finely chopped
1 clove garlic, finely chopped
750ml Vegetable or Chicken Stock
1 red chilli, deseeded and finely chopped, or 2 tsp chilli paste
800g Frozen peas
50g 5% Fat Soft cheese (Philadelphia Extra Light)
200g Smoked Pancetta finely diced.

Method

Heat the olive oil in a large pot, add in the onion and the garlic and cook until the onion is softened but not browned.
Add the chilli and cook for a further two minutes.
Add the stock and bring to the boil.
Add the peas and cook for 4-5 minutes.
Transfer the mix to a blender and pulse until smooth.
Return the soup to the pot and add the cheese and stir until blended.
Meanwhile fry the smoked pancetta and drain off any excess oil and add to the soup.
This gives a thick and creamy soup but if it is too thick more stock can be added.
The more chilli you use the more bite you get....

A domestic goddess I ain't, I'm afraid, you will never find me slaving over a hot stove or fretting over last minute preparations for a fancy dinner party. That said I'm known to whip up the odd homemade soup or hearty stew or throw-it-all-in casserole. They're nutritious and tasty and perfect for lazy cooks like me. Enjoy.

Sharon Ní Bheoláin
Irish television newsreader with RTÉ. Today, she is best known as co-anchor of RTÉ One's RTÉ News: Six One

Recipe for Disaster

ALL PROCEEDS IN AID OF IRISH ORTHOPAEDIC HAITI FUND

Main Course Recipes

Ian Dempsey's Swedish Meatballs (Kottbullar)

Ingredients (Serves 4)

1 Onion – peeled and finely chopped
50g Butter
200ml Whipping Cream
50g white breadcrumbs
200g minced beef
200g minced pork
1 egg beaten
Half a teaspoon of All Spice
Salt and white pepper

And for the cream gravy
1 medium onion – peeled and chopped
1 medium carrot – peeled and chopped
2 small sticks of celery - chopped
275 ml of chicken stock
1 tablespoon of redcurrant jelly
A generous pinch of All Spice
150 ml of whipping cream
A handful of (frozen) cranberries
Salt and white pepper

Method

Sauté the onion in half the butter and then leave it on a plate to cool down.
Pour the cream over the breadcrumbs in a bowl and let it mix in before adding the cooled onion, the minced pork and the minced beef.
Add the egg, All Spice, salt and white pepper and mix it all up with your hands.
When it's all mixed up make up small meatballs about the size of a walnut.
Gently fry the meatballs on a pan using the remaining butter until they are golden and cooked through.
Put the cooked meatballs aside while you make the gravy
Now, fry the onion, carrot and celery until they are tender.
Transfer them to a saucepan, pour in the chicken stock and simmer until the liquid has reduced by about a half.
Using a sieve, strain the liquid into a clean frying pan large enough to take the meatballs later.
Stir in the redcurrant jelly and then season with All Spice, salt & white pepper.
When the jelly has dissolved, add the cream and stir it into the mixture.
Now, the meatballs are mixed in with a handful of cranberries to make it more colourful. Leave it all on the hob for about 2 minutes and then serve it up.
Peas, small diced roast potatoes and red cabbage are good with this dish – and maybe a small glass of chilled Schnapps – oh go on.

With IKEA now firmly established in Ireland, you could pop out to Ballymun and buy all of this ready made and frozen – but making it from scratch is much nicer – and you'll feel a lot better about yourself too!

Ian Dempsey Popular Irish Television and Breakfast radio presenter.
He is the current present of Ireland's Today FM's radio breakfast show

Recipe for Disaster

ALL PROCEEDS IN AID OF IRISH ORTHOPAEDIC HAITI FUND

Chicken, Chorizo and Pasta Dish

Ingredients

3 tbsp olive oil
2-3 garlic cloves, sliced
2 tins of tomatoes
handful of basil leaves
2 red peppers, chopped
1 red onion, chopped

1 red chilli (optional)
3 chicken breasts, chopped
200g chorizo
handful of parmesan cheese, grated
penne

Method

Heat the olive oil and garlic over a low heat in a saucepan. Add in the
tomatoes, peppers, onion and chilli (if using). Season
with salt, pepper and some sugar. Cover and cook gently for 10
minutes, then purée to make your sauce. Shred the basil leaves
and add to the sauce.
Meanwhile, cook your meat. Stir fry the chopped chicken
breasts in a frying pan with some olive oil, and when cooked
add in to the sauce. Give the pan a wipe, and when the pan is
hot add the sliced chorizo. Cook the slices for one minute or so
on each side.
Add the chorizo to your sauce, along with the cooked penne.
Toss it all together, and sprinkle with some freshly grated
Parmesan to serve.

*This is a recipe for chicken, chorizo and pasta dinner I have during the
week before training*

Paul Griffin Dublin Gaelic Footballer

Old Missus Mooney's Chicken Ala King

Ingredients

Four chicken breasts
8 medium size potatoes
(2 spuds per person)
3 mixed peppers
(Green, Yellow and Red)
1 large onion

Mushrooms - mixed varieties - Button,
Chanterelle, Oyster. Whatever takes
your fancy.
Half glass of wine
Fresh pouring cream
Salt and Pepper for seasoning

Method

Peel the potatoes and do your best to ensure that each potato is the
same size. Doing this will ensure that they will all be cooked
at same time.
Cut all four chicken breasts into bite size chunks.
Clean and slice the peppers the onions and the mushrooms.
Preheat oven at 200 Celsius.
Place potatoes in saucepan and cook for 25 minutes.
Fry the chicken until meat is white and cooked through, this should take
about five minutes. When Chicken is cooked place in Pyrex dish and stick in the
oven. Clean the frying pan then cook the onions, then the peppers
and finally the mushrooms.
Place onions, peppers and mushrooms into a large frying pan or WOK.
Take the chicken from the oven and add. Season with salt and pepper.
Add a half glass of white wine and leave to simmer for approximately 10
minutes.
Just before serving, pour in fresh cream and stir.
To get the best mash potatoes, season with salt, add milk and cream
then mash.
Present each guest with a plate of mashed potato, then serve each diner
a healthy portion of Old Missus Mooney's Chicken Ala King

*One of the first dishes I made when I first began to cook was Chicken Ala King. I
call it Old Missus Mooney's Chicken Ala King, not because my mother used to
make it, come to think of it she never made it, but because Old Missus Mooney's
Chicken Ala king has a nice ring to it and by adding the Old Missus Mooney bit, it
has character too. I usually do this dish when I have friends over to watch TV. It's
not fussy, it's really tasty and it's not really Chicken Ala King, as you will discover.
By the way this recipe is genuinely my own and will serve four people, depending
on the portions you dish up. Enjoy!*

Derek Mooney Irish radio and television personallity as well as a radio producer

Recipe for Disaster

ALL PROCEEDS IN AID OF IRISH ORTHOPAEDIC HAITI FUND

Chilli Con Carne

Ingredients (Serves 3-4)

500g minced pork
400g tomatoes (chopped)
200g red kidney beans
(tinned beans more convenient)
400g brown rice
2 tablespoons sunflower oil

1 red onion (chopped)
1 clove garlic (crushed)
1 level teaspoon crushed chillies
Jalapeno peppers to taste
Salt and pepper

Method

Heat the oil in a pan over medium heat. Add the mince, chopped onion, crushed garlic, pepper, jalapenos and crushed chilli.
Once meat is golden brown, add the tomatoes and kidney beans.
Stir until heated thoroughly.
Add the brown rice to boiling water and allow to simmer until rice softens to taste (brown rice is firmer than white rice,).
Serve hot with a cold beer!

I enjoy this meal because it is quick to prepare, low in fat and easily varied from mild to "muy picante!!" depending on your mood.
Brown rice is higher in fibre than white rice, and has a sweet, nutty taste to offset the spicy chilli.

Aaron Glynn Orthopaedic Registrar (Haiti February 2010)

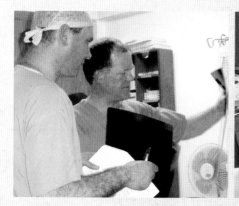
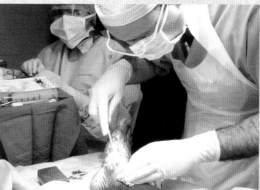

Recipe *for* Disaster

ALL PROCEEDS IN AID OF IRISH ORTHOPAEDIC HAITI FUND

Stir Fry Chicken

Ingredients

2 chicken breasts
cornflower
soya sauce
sherry
oyster sauce
chicken stock
peppers
carrots
onion
courgette
beansprouts
mange tout
garlic
salt and pepper

Method

Marinade chicken - cut chicken into thin strips,
add 1 teaspoon of cornflower, 2 teaspoons of sherry, 2 teaspoons of oyster sauce,
1 teaspoon of soya, pinch sugar, salt and pepper. Mix around and
leave in Tupperware container.

Next get 7oz chicken stock, add 2 teaspoons of cornflower, 4 teaspoons soya
sauce, mix and leave to side
Chop all vegetables.
Heat wok with oil, put the veg into the wok and cook for a couple of minutes.
Leave the veg on a warmed plate.
Add more oil to the wok cook chicken, brown it, pour stock and bubble it while
still stirring.
Add veg, mix around and it is done.
Serve as I suggest above with egg noodles (my favourite) or rice.

*Not that I do much cooking anymore but one of my few dishes would be a
straight forward chicken stir fry served with egg noodles or rice. Easy to do and
great to eat after watching everyone training hard!!!*

**Conor O'Shea former Ruby Union player who played at full back for Ireland,
Lansdowne R.F.C. & London Irish. He is the director of Rugby at Harrlequins F.C.
and Rugby presenter.**

Thai Ginger Sea Bass with Mushrooms and Lime

Ingredients

15g dried mushrooms,
such as shiitake or cup
40g cornflour, plus extra 1 tbsp
1 tbsp Thai fish sauce
2 tbsp dark soy sauce
3 tbsp Billington's Light Muscovado Sugar
2 tbsp lime juice
Sunflower oil, for deep frying
4 x 175-200g sea bass fillets, scaled
and pin- boned

2 fat garlic cloves, thinly sliced
1 medium-hot red chilli, deseeded and sliced
5cm piece of ginger,
cut into fine matchsticks
6 spring onions, trimmed, halved and finely
shredded
Fresh coriander sprigs, to garnish

Method

Cover the mushrooms with 175ml hot water and soak for 20 minutes.
Drain, reserving the water, and thinly slice the mushrooms. Mix the extra 1 tbsp
cornflour with 3 tbsp of the reserved water.
Put the rest of the water into a small pan with the fish sauce, soy, sugar and lime
juice. Bring to a simmer, add the cornflour mixture and simmer for 1 minute until
thickened and smooth. Keep on a low heat.
Pour 1cm of oil into a large, deep frying pan and heat to 190°C (if you don't have
a thermometer, it will be ready when a cube of bread takes 30 seconds to turn
golden). Sift the remaining cornflour onto a baking tray. Season the fish on both
sides with a little salt, then coat in the cornflour and pat off the excess. When the
oil is ready, add the sea bass fillets skin-side up and shallow-fry for 1 minute.
Turn, fry for a further minute, then lift onto a baking tray lined with kitchen paper
and keep warm in a low oven.
Heat 11/2 tbsp of oil in a medium-sized frying pan or wok.
Add the garlic and, as soon as it starts to turn golden, add the chilli and ginger
and stir-fry for a further 30 seconds. Add the mushrooms and half the spring
onions and stir-fry for 1 minute.
Lift the fish onto warmed plates and spoon over some of the sauce.
Scatter with the fried mushrooms and spring onions and garnish with the remaining shredded spring onions and plenty of coriander sprigs. Serve with some plain
steamed rice.

I have always LOVED Thai Ginger sea bass.
Hope this is ok: it's a great healthy option and so easy to do at
home. I usually try to eat fish when I'm eating out but this is now a
regular in my own kitchen.

Brian O'Driscoll Irish and Leinster Rugby Star

Recipe for Disaster

ALL PROCEEDS IN AID OF IRISH ORTHOPAEDIC HAITI FUND

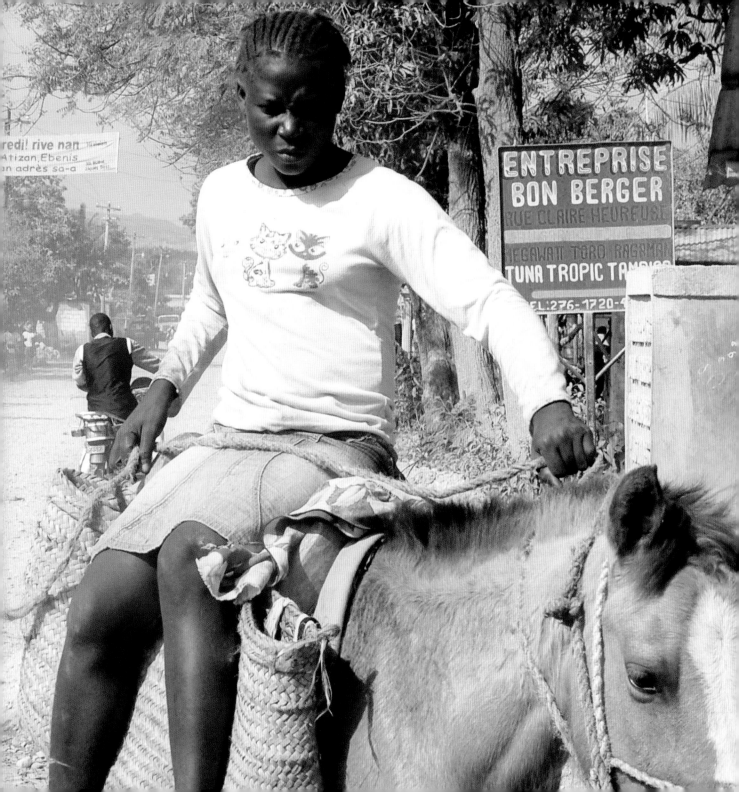

Spaghetti Bolognaise

Ingredients

1 lb lean minced beef
1 onion
Handful of mushrooms
1 red pepper
1 clove garlic, crushed
2 tins of chopped tomatoes
2 tbsp of tomato purée
1 red chilli, finely chopped
1 tbsp of Olive oil
Salt and pepper to season

Spaghetti
Parmesan cheese
Black pepper

Method

Brown the mince in olive oil.
Add the chopped onion, mushrooms and red pepper. Cook until all are soft.
Pour in the chopped tomatoes and tomato purée
Bring to the boil and simmer for 30 minutes
Serve with Spaghetti, Parmesan cheese and black pepper

Ruby Walsh
Professional jockey, who, to date had ridden over fourteen hundred winners. He is currently the reigning Irish National Hunt champion jockey.

Recipe for Disaster
ALL PROCEEDS IN AID OF IRISH ORTHOPAEDIC HAITI FUND

Chicken Pieces in The Oven

Ingredients

1 whole chicken chopped into 6 or 8 pieces by your butcher. (You can also use chicken pieces but best if you can have some bones and skin to keep the chicken moist and tasty)
8- 10 large plum tomatoes – quartered
7-8 cloves of garlic – skin on
Plenty of basil leaves- torn
Salt and pepper and a good splash of olive oil

Method

Heat the oven to 200°C.
Arrange the chicken in a casserole dish in one layer. Put the garlic cloves between the chicken pieces and lots of torn basil leaves.
Quarter the tomatoes and scatter loosely amongst the chicken pieces. Season with salt and pepper and splash of olive oil.
Put in the oven for 20 minutes then turn temperature down to 180°c for about an hour, check near the bones to ensure the chicken is cooked, if unsure leave for an extra 20 minutes.
Serve with crispy roast potatoes and peas or your favourite green vegetable.

This is my favourite recipe, mainly because it is so simple and requires very little attention once prepared.

Sonia O'Sullivan
One of the worlds leading female athletes for most of the 1990's and early first decade of the 21st century

Recipe for Disaster
ALL PROCEEDS IN AID OF IRISH ORTHOPAEDIC HAITI FUND

Frittata with Oven Roasted Tomatoes, Chorizo and Ardsallagh Goat's Cheese

Ingredients (Serves 6)

450g (1lb) ripe or sun-blushed tomatoes, preferably cherry tomatoes
1 teaspoon salt and freshly ground black pepper
8 large eggs, preferably free range and organic
2 tablespoons (2 American tablespoons + 2 teaspoons) parsley, chopped
4 teaspoons thyme leaves
2 tablespoons (2 American tablespoons + 2 teaspoons) basil, mint or marjoram
110-175g (4-6oz) chorizo, thickly sliced, cut into four
40g (1 1/2ozs) Parmesan cheese, grated
25g (1oz/1/4 stick) butter
110g (4oz) soft goat's cheese (We use Ardsallagh goat cheese)
Extra virgin olive oil
Non-stick pan 10cm (7 1/2in) bottom, 23cm (9in) top rim

Method

Preheat the oven to 180°C/350°F/gas mark 4.
Cut the tomatoes in half around the equator season with salt and a few grinds of pepper. Arrange in a single layer in a non-stick roasting tin. Roast for 10-15 or until almost soft and slightly crinkly. Remove from the heat and cool. Alternatively use sun-blushed tomatoes.
Whisk the eggs in a bowl; add the salt, freshly ground pepper, fresh herbs, chorizo and grated cheese into the eggs. Add the tomatoes and stir gently.
Melt the butter in a non-stick frying pan. When the butter starts to foam, tip in the eggs. Turn down the heat, as low as it will go. Divide the cheese into walnut sized pieces and drop gently into the frittata at regular intervals. Leave the eggs to cook gently for 15 minutes on a heat diffuser mat, or until the underneath is set. The top should still be slightly runny.
Preheat a grill. Pop the pan under the grill for 1 minute to set and barely brown the surface.
Slide the frittata onto a warm plate.
Serve cut in wedges with a good green salad and perhaps a few olives.
Alternatively put the pan into a preheated oven 170°C/325°F/gas 3.
Alternatively cook mini frittata in muffin tins (for approximately 15 minutes).
Serve with a good green salad.

Variation: For a yummy vegetarian alternative omit the chorizo and add 110g (4oz) grated Gruyère cheese to add extra zizz.

Top Tip

The size of the pan is very important, the frittata should be at least 3 cm (1 1/4 inches) thick. It the only pan available is larger adjust the number of eggs etc.

"Frittata is an Italian omelette. Kuku and Spanish tortilla all sounds much more exciting than a flat omelette although that is basically what they are. Unlike their soft and creamy French cousin, these omelettes are cooked slowly over a very low heat during which time you can be whipping up a delicious salad to accompany it! A frittata is cooked gently on both sides and cut into wedges like a piece of cake. Omit the tomato and you have a basic recipe, flavoured with grated cheese and a generous sprinkling of herbs. Like the omelette, though, you'll occasionally want to add some tasty morsels however, to ring the changes perhaps some spinach, ruby chard, Calabreze, asparagus, smoked mackerel, etc. The list is endless but be careful don't use it as a dustbin - think about the combination of flavours before you empty your fridge!"

Darina Allen Ballymaloe Cookery School
An Irish Chef, TV personality and founder of Ballymaloe Cookery School

MAIN COURSES

Indonesian Style Chicken Couscous

Ingredients
300g couscous
1 large red pepper, deseeded and diced
9 tbsp crunchy peanut butter
2 large chicken breasts chopped into strips
1 bunch of spring onions, trimmed and finely sliced

Method
Put the couscous and red pepper into a large bowl.
Measure 350ml boiling water into a jug, stir in 3 tbsp of the peanut butter, and stir the mixture into the couscous. Cover with cling film and set aside for 5 minutes, until the liquid has been absorbed. Fluff up with a fork.
Meanwhile, fry the chicken strips.
Add the spring onions to the couscous, along with the chicken. Toss together, season to taste and divide between plates.
Put the remaining peanut butter in a bowl and gradually stir in 6 tbsp hot water, to thin down. Drizzle over the couscous to serve.

Jamie Heaslip Irish and Leinster Rugby Star

Jayo's Sweet Potato Shepherd's Pie

Ingredients

450g of lamb mince
3 carrots (Diced)
2 onions (Diced)
1 garlic clove (Minced)
100g of peas
1pt of stock (chicken)
1 tbsp of Dijon mustard
1 tsp of tomato purée
2 sweet potatoes (peeled)
3 potatoes (peeled)
30g of butter

Method

Fry the garlic, onion and carrots in a pan until browned, add the lamb mince and brown together. Add the peas, then the Dijon mustard, tomato purée and mix. Add the chicken stock and simmer for 20 minutes.
Meanwhile boil the potatoes and the sweet potato, combine both when cooked with a little butter and mash.
Spread meat mixture in an ovenproof dish and top with the potato. Cook in a pre-heated oven at 180 °c for 20 minutes until the potato is golden brown.

I like my comfort food but when you are playing sport you have to try and eat healthily, to me this is the ultimate healthy comfort food! Ensure to serve in big dishes, second helpings are recommended, enjoy!

Jason Sherlock
Former Irish Gaelic Footballer who played for Dublin between 1995 and 2010

Recipe for Disaster

ALL PROCEEDS IN AID OF IRISH ORTHOPAEDIC HAITI FUND

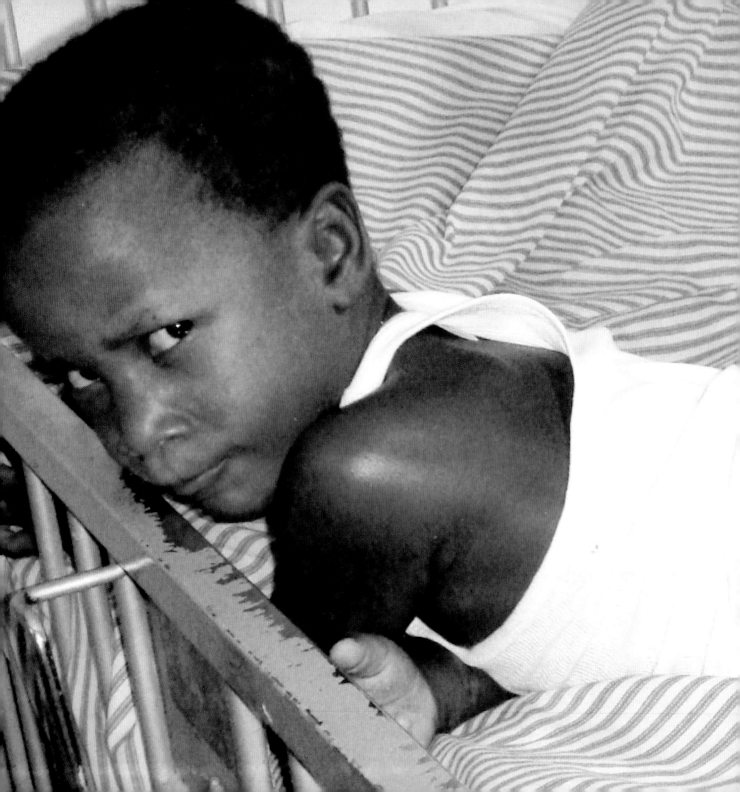

Irish Stew with Dumplings

Ingredients
Stew
1kg (2 lbs) shoulder of lamb, well trimmed and diced (keep bones)
2 carrots chopped
1 onion chopped
1 white turnip chopped
2 sticks of celery chopped
1 leek finely chopped
Salt and pepper
2ozs cabbage finely chopped
1/4/ pint of cream
Chopped parsley, fresh thyme, bay leaf
4-6 potatoes
Dumplings
4ozs of self-raising flour
1 tablespoon of fresh parsley
2ozs shredded suet.
Method
Place meat in a pot and cover with cold salted water.
Bring to the boil, then drain and rinse.
Peel and chop onions, carrots, white turnip, celery, leek and cabbage.
In a fresh pot put the meat, bones, vegetables, bouquet of herbs and seasoning.
Cover with water and simmer gently for 1 hour, skimming off scum as it rises.
Peel potatoes and cut into chunks, then add to pot, continue cooking
for 25 minutes. Shred cabbage and add to pot for the last 5 minutes. About 15
minutes before the end of cooking time make the dumplings.
To make dumplings mix the flour, salt, pepper, parsley and suet in a bowl. It must
not be rubbed in. Add just enough cold water to make a fairly stiff but elastic
dough. Shape into 8 dumplings.
When the stew is ready remove the meat and veg. Cover and keep warm. Season
the liquid to taste, and then bring to the boil.
Place the dumplings into the pot and cover and cook for 20-25 minutes – do not
let them come off the boil. Serve the meat surrounded by the vegetables and
dumplings, add chopped parsley and cream to the liquid and pour over. Serve
remainder in a gravy boat.
Babs Keating *"My favourite dish"*
Retired Irish hurling manager and former player. He played hurling with Tipperary
senior inter-county team in the 1960's & 1970's

Chicken Fricassee

Ingredients
1lb Chicken Fillets (strips)
1 Onion (finely chopped)
½ pint water
2 tsp lemon juice
Seasoning
Pinch mixed herbs
½ pint white sauce.

Method
Simmer chicken, onion, mixed herbs, seasoning and water together for
1 hour or less.
Strain off liquid and make up to ½ pint with milk.
Make a white sauce (1/2 oz flour & 1/2 oz margarine) using this
liquid in place of milk.
Season with lemon juice, salt and pepper.
Add chicken & onions and reheat.
Serve garnished with cooked mushroom slices, bacon rolls and lemon slices.

Noel Dempsey
Fianna Fáil Politician. Current Minister for Transport

Recipe for Disaster

ALL PROCEEDS IN AID OF IRISH ORTHOPAEDIC HAITI FUND

Chicken Ding

Ingredients

1 large breast of chicken
1 tsp of Olive oil
1 tsp of Cajun spice

Method

Coat chicken with oil olive and then roll in Cajun spice.
Place chicken on a microwave proof plate.
Place chicken in microwave.
Set microwave to 'COOK' for 5 minutes.
Turn chicken and the set microwave to 'COOK' for another 5 minutes.
Wait for the DING and then remove from the microwave.
Serve with a salad.

Jonathon Sexton
Irish and Leinster Rugby Star

Chicken Fried Rice

Ingredients (Serves 2)

4 normal sized chicken breasts
2 portions rice
2 eggs
1 chopped onion
1 courgette
Mushrooms to your taste
Garlic butter
Soya sauce

Method

Steam the rice.
Chop chicken breasts and cook on the wok, remove and set aside.
Cook all the vegetables in garlic butter in the wok and add back in the chicken.
Sprinkle with soy sauce to your taste.
Add boiled rice to the top and break 2 eggs over it, stir the mixture until egg is cooked and everything is well mixed.
Serve immediately.

Padraig Harrington
Irish professional golfer. He has won three major championships:
The Open Championship in 2007 & 2008 and PGA Championship, also in 2008.

Recipe for Disaster
ALL PROCEEDS IN AID OF IRISH ORTHOPAEDIC HAITI FUND

Chicken & Avocado Greek Salad

Ingredients (serves 2-4)
2 Chicken breasts
1 ripe Avocado
1 lemon
1 tsp dried Oregano
½ red onion
1 small Cos lettuce
150g feta cheese
½ small loaf of ciabatta bread
Red wine vinegar
Extra virgin olive oil
Salt and pepper

Method
Grill the chicken breasts under medium heat until golden and cooked through. Slice and set aside.

Cut the crusts off the ciabatta and discard, and then tear up the remaining into thumb size pieces. Toast on medium heat grill pan until crisp and lightly charred. Turn heat off and set aside.

Stone Avocado then cut each half in half again lengthways. Peel off skin & slice the quarters across into ½ cm slices & place in a large mixing bowl.

Grate the lemon zest into a small bowl, cut lemon in half then squeeze in the juice from one half.

Squeeze some of the other half of lemon over the Avocado, then toss (this will stop avocado turning brown)

Sprinkle ½ tsp of the oregano plus 2 tsp of olive oil into the lemon juice. Add pinch of salt and pepper. Peel and finely slice the onion and place it in another small bowl with a splash of red wine vinegar and pinch of salt and pepper.

Wash and spin dry lettuce leaves and tear into bite-sized pieces. Add to avocado bowl.

Stir dressing and pour onto lettuce and avocado mix.

Add onion mix, warm toasted bread and sliced chicken. Toss everything and divide between two plates. Crumb feta over top of salad, drizzle a little olive oil and sprinkle rest of oregano on top.

David Wallace Irish and Munster Rugby Star

Oven Baked Cod Fillet

Ingredients
Cod fish fillets of a thickness of 3cm are preferable.

Method
Flatten tinfoil onto a shallow baking dish, leaving sufficient "spare" foil to cover the dish.

Wipe vegetable or olive oil onto the tinfoil in the dish. Place a sprig of dill onto the foil.

Place a thick fillet of cod skin side down on the bottom of the dish and place another sprig of dill and some shavings of full butter on top.

Close the tinfoil cocoon style and place the tray in a preheated (200°C) oven for 15 minutes.

Any fish from smoked coley (probably my favourite) to halibut can be done this way.

The thickness of the fish will determine the cooking time. Whole fish (including the head!) are particularly succulent when cooked this way.

Use a little parsley sauce or packet fish sauce if required. Serve with rice or small new potatoes.

Vegetable suggestions include steamed green beans, broccoli, peas, leeks, fennel and spinach.

With fish, cooking time is crucial, so adjust time accordingly.

A good dry or semi-dry white wine would be essential!

Kevin Conneff
More familiarly known as the voice, rhythmic heartbeat, and the bodhrán player of the legendary Irish folk group The Chieftains.

Podge & Rodge's Coddle

Ingredients

1lb/500g sausages
8oz/250g streaky bacon
½ pint/ 300ml stock (or water if the recession is still on)
6 potatoes (about the size of a lady's clenched fist)
2 onions (as above size wise. If you don't have a lady's fist to hand, just buy medium sized ones)
Seasoning (that's salt and pepper to us)

Method

Cut the bacon into 1inch pieces. You can use your teeth but a knife is better.
Bring the stock to the boil in a pan, throw in the sausages and the bacon and boil for around 5 minutes.
Take out the meat, and save the liquid. You can pour it into a bowl or an old chamber pot like granny used to do.
At this stage, the sausages will be the consistency of fingers after staying in the bath too long. Cut them into quarters.
Peel the potatoes and chop into thick slices. Peel the onions and slice them.
Assemble half the potatoes and onions in layers, and then add half the bacon and sausages. Repeat and finish with a layer of potatoes. Pour the stock back over and add some salt and pepper. Cover the pan and simmer gently for about an hour.
Serve with thick slices of buttered bread. Now that's a proper meal!

Back in our day, we didn't have poncey cooking methods like stir-frying, steaming or sauté-ing what ever that is. No, there were only three methods of cooking: frying, boiling or sticking it in the oven, and all good recipes only ever had a handful of ingredients. No pinches of foreign herbs, or tomatoes sun dried on a roof in Mumbai. So when we were asked to give a recipe to this book, we thought we'd give a proper Irish recipe. O'Casey swore by it, and Joyce wrote about it so if that's not good enough for you, nothing is. Also, apart from crisp sandwiches, it's the only recipe we know. Just make sure you use Irish ingredients mind. No point in us giving you a traditional Irish recipe if you go buying some fancy foreign rashers from acorn fed pigs or what have you. This will serve four people by today's standards, but would have served a family of twelve and a dog back in 1950.

Paudge and Rodge Broadcast Entertainers

Recipe for Disaster

ALL PROCEEDS IN AID OF IRISH ORTHOPAEDIC HAITI FUND

Poached Salmon with Asparagus Salad, New Season Potatoes and Lemon Mayonnaise

Ingredients

2.5kg/5lb 6oz whole salmon,
scaled and gutted
1 onion
2 bay leaves
4 tbsp white wine vinegar
1 lemon, quartered
salt and freshly ground black pepper
For the Salad
24 asparagus spears
3 tbsp olive oil
6 thick slices white bread,
cut into 1cm/½in cubes
2 sprigs fresh rosemary
½tsp Dijon mustard

1 tbsp white wine vinegar
3 tbsp extra virgin olive oil
2 heads baby Little Gem lettuce,
leaves separated
For the mayonnaise
2 large free-range egg yolks
1 tsp white wine vinegar
½tsp mustard powder
1 tsp salt
1 lemon, juice only
275ml/10fl oz rapeseed oil
salt and freshly ground black pepper

6/8 Small New Season Potatoes (Boiled)

Method

Place the salmon in a large roasting tin and pour in enough cold water to cover the fish. Add the onion, bay leaves, vinegar, lemon and a good pinch of salt and freshly ground black pepper. Cover with a lid or tin foil and bring to the boil. Once at a boil, turn off the heat and leave the fish to stand in the water until it has cooled to room temperature.

For the salad, toss the asparagus spears with one tablespoon of the olive oil and season with salt and black pepper. Fry for 2-3 minutes on a hot pan until charred and just tender. Add to other salad ingredients

Mayonnaise

Whisk eggs.
Add Vinegar, mustard powder, salt & whisk again.
Slowly add the rapeseed oil and continue to whisk slowly until the mixture is cream like.
Add lemon juice

A light, healthy summer dish.

John Tracey Former Olympic medalist and current Irish Sports Council CEO

Recipe for Disaster

ALL PROCEEDS IN AID OF IRISH ORTHOPAEDIC HAITI FUND

Beef Stroganoff

Ingredients

1 lb fillet steak, cut into thin strips
2 teaspoons vegetable oil
1 onion, chopped.
8 ounces sliced mushrooms
2 oz full cream
1 Garlic clove, chopped.
1 tsp paprika.
2–3 flat-leaf parsley sprigs, chopped
Knob of butter

Method

Cut the beef into finger-width slices. Season with salt, pepper & paprika.
Heat oil in a large pan over medium heat. Fry the onion and garlic till softened.
Turn up heat and add the mushrooms and butter, sautéing until the mushroom are golden brown, and put aside.
Add oil to the pan; fry the beef for 2 minutes until brown. Stir in the mushroom & onion mixture for 1 minute.
Remove from heat and stir in the cream and parsley. Serve with rice.

My Favourite Recipe. This is a quick and easy,
very filling and rich meal to be followed by a trip to the gym!

Ben Dunne Irish Entrepreneur

Roast Belly of Pork

Ingredients

2 kg raw pork belly
250g butter
1 large onion
3 cloves of garlic

200g fresh sage
500g fresh breadcrumbs
salt and pepper for seasoning

Method

Turn pork skin side down on the board. Make an incision ¾ way down the flesh so that there is a flap to fold back over the stuffing. Put to one side.

Finely dice onion and crush the garlic. Put pot on the stove on low heat. Add the butter and all the diced onion. Cook out the onion until translucent and add the crushed garlic. Once garlic begins to cook add breadcrumbs mixing thoroughly and remove from heat. Chop sage finely and add to mix.

Fold out the pork and season the meat, place breadcrumb mix down the centre of the pork. Pull flesh over top of breadcrumb mix. Tie with butcher twine from end to end.

Put six layers of cling-film on the work surface, place pork close to the edge and roll up tightly in sausage like fashion. Tie at one end, squeezing the air out and then tie at the other end. Cut off any excess cling-film and wrap with another four layers.

Place in a pot of simmering water for up to three hours. Put weight on top of meat to avoid buoyancy and to ensure the pork is cooked through.

Once complete remove cling film and trim the rind off the meat to reveal soft fat. Put a frying pan on the heat, place joint on the pan and brown evenly. Finish in oven at 180° for 10 minutes. Take out and allow to rest for 10 minutes, carve and serve.

Roy Moffett Chef

MAIN COURSES

Recipe for Disaster

ALL PROCEEDS IN AID OF IRISH ORTHOPAEDIC HAITI FUND

75

Honey Roast Ham (The Steed/Hayes Way)

Firstly go to your local butcher and purchase a nice piece of fillet of ham, and get him/her to skin it leaving only a thin layer of fat, and then re-string for you. You may need to soak the ham overnight depending on salt content, I always do.

Ingredients
Fillet of ham
Cloves
7upfree
Honey
"Magic" Turkey Roasting Bag (this is actually the key)

Method

Score the fat on the ham in a nice crisscross design and stick a clove in each cross.
Place the ham into the extra large bag, resting in roasting tray and cover generously with honey.
Pour in a generous amount of 7up free to the base of the bag.
Tie bag with little tie thing. Pierce bag once or twice.
Place in roasting oven of Aga or preheated conventional oven 200°.
Depending on size of ham, cook for 1.5 to 2 hours (half ham) or 2.5 to 3 hours (full ham).
After 1.5 hours (half ham) remove from bag and drain bag safely.
Place ham back on tray and add a little extra honey to the top.
This allows top to crisp and adds to taste.
I usually cook the ham the night before as we feel it tastes better cold and it gets all the mess out of the way. Can be served with some homegrown carrots, turnips and potatoes all cooked in the simmering oven of the Aga.
Or alternatively a selection of roast vegetables cooked in baking tray with squeezed lemon, garlic, rosemary and a drizzle of olive oil. We do always tend to have some mash!
We don't really use sauces or gravies but people could add sauce of choice.

John Hayes Irish and Munster Rugby star
Fiona Steed Former Irish Women's Rugby International player

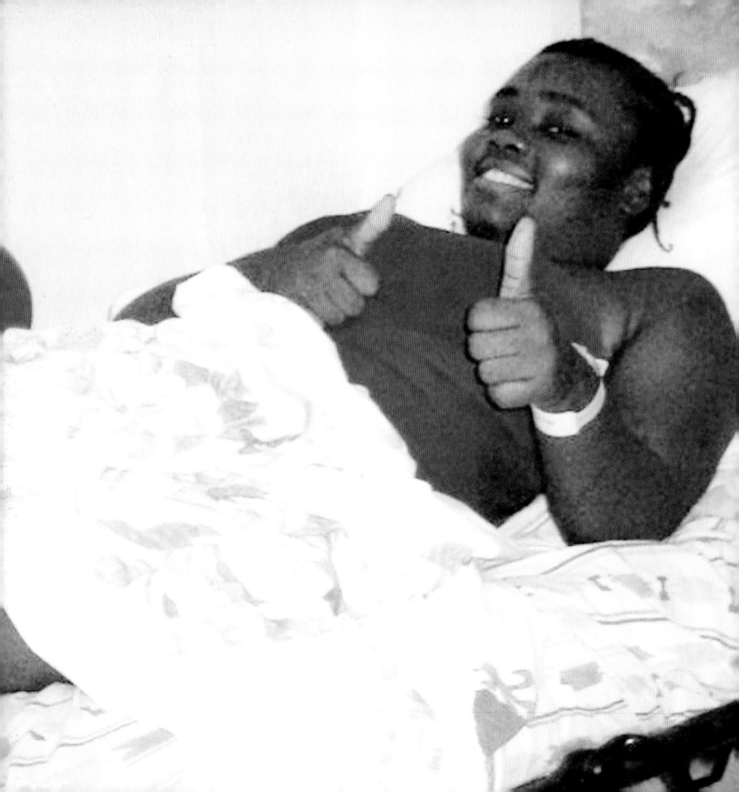

Mechado (Filipino Beef Stew)

Ingredients (Serves 2)
1 k.g beef (cut into pieces)
cooking oil
4 cloves garlic (crushed)
1 onion (sliced)
2 potatoes (quartered, fried)
1 carrot (cut round)
2 tbsp lemon juice
2 tbsp soy sauce, salt, peppercorn
1 cup tomato sauce
1 pc. Laurel
hot water

Method
Brown meat in cooking oil. Set aside.
In same oil sauté garlic and onion. Add lemon, soy sauce, peppercorn, tomato sauce, laurel and salt, simmer for a few minutes then add water. Cover and simmer. Add potatoes and carrot when meat is tender

Josie Nacpil Theatre Nurse (Haiti February 2010)

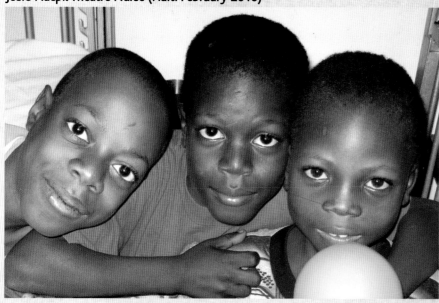

Recipe for Disaster

ALL PROCEEDS IN AID OF IRISH ORTHOPAEDIC HAITI FUND

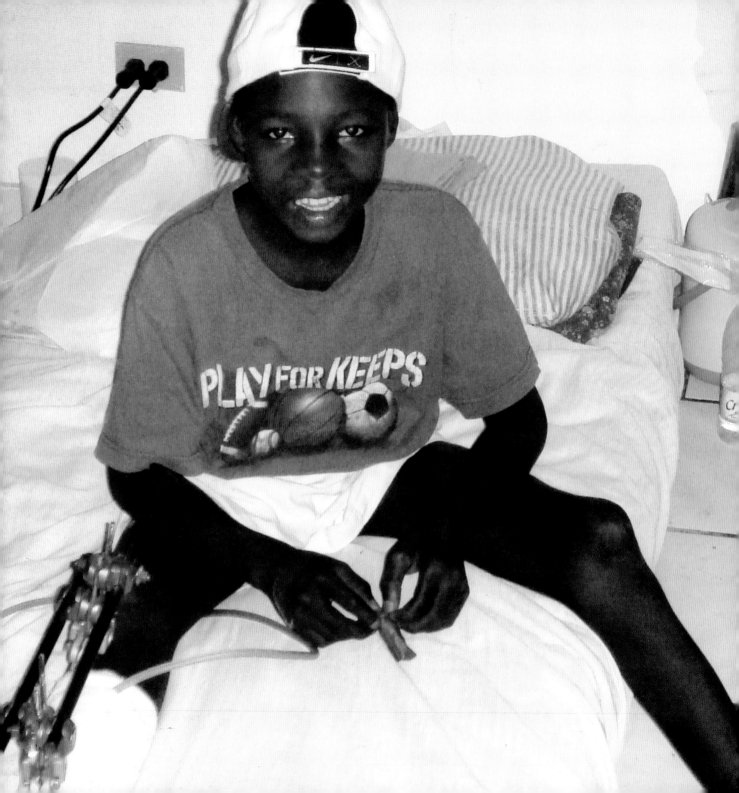

Tripe and Onions – Cork Style by George Hook

Ingredients (Serves: 4)

450 Gram Dressed tripe, washed (1 lb)
Potatoes to taste.
3 Medium Onions, sliced
600 ml Milk (1 pint)
Pinch Grated nutmeg

1 Bayleaf (optional)
25 Gram Butter (1 oz)
3 Tablespoon Plain flour
Fresh parsley, chopped for garnish

Method

Put the tripe in a saucepan and cover with cold water. Bring to the boil, then drain and rinse under cold running water. Cut into 2.5 cm (1 inch) pieces.

Put the tripe, milk, nutmeg and bay leaf (if using) in the rinsed out pan. Bring to the boil, cover and simmer for about 2 hours, until tender. Strain off the liquid and reserve 600 ml (1 pint).

Melt the butter in a saucepan, stir in the flour and cook gently for 1 minute, stirring. Remove the pan from the heat and gradually stir in the reserved cooking liquid. Bring to the boil and continue to cook, stirring, until the sauce thickens. Add the tripe, onions and potatoes and reheat. Serve sprinkled with parsley.

Notes to make it work like my Mother used to do.

Clean the tripe about a dozen times under cool water to remove any "undesirable" elements.

Allow the tripe to simmer, stirring all the while to keep the bottom of the pot from burning.

Check every twenty minutes for tenderness. There is a certain balance giving, but not falling apart.

The lovely Ingrid said that it reminded her of beef stroganoff, and I can see where she is coming from. The tripe itself was nice and tender—a little chewy in places—but you could cut it with a spoon.

Do not let the word tripe deter you, let its soothing charms win you over and enjoy it as do those who always have! Visually, as well as gastronomically, there is a great serenity to a plate of tripe and onions.
Tripe and onions was an inexpensive and filling dish of my youth in Cork. Honeycomb tripe is best and comes from the second stomach of the cow. A trip to the English Market in Cork is recommended for the very best tripe.
I've waxed poetic about tripe a few times before. However, following a cookbook directions exactly, using the best possible ingredients, it can still end up being terrible.

George Hook Irish broadcaster, Journalist & Rugby Union Pundit

Recipe for Disaster

ALL PROCEEDS IN AID OF IRISH ORTHOPAEDIC HAITI FUND

Recipe for Disaster

ALL PROCEEDS IN AID OF IRISH ORTHOPAEDIC HAITI FUND

Vegetarian Bobotie

Ingredients (Serves 4)

1 tbsp olive oil
2 large onions, finely chopped
3 garlic cloves, crushed
1 cup / 240 ml milk
3 or 4 slices white bread, stale with crusts removed
2.5cm piece fresh ginger, grated
2 tbsp curry powder
1 tsp ground cumin
1 tsp ground coriander
½ tsp freshly grated black pepper

3/4 cup dried apricots, chopped (or otherwise apricot jam)
2 tbsp sultanas (better than raisins which can make the dish too sweet)
½ cup almonds, chopped
1 dessert apple, peeled and grated
4 tbsp lemon juice
1 cup red lentils, washed
1 can black-eyed beans, drained
3 tbsp parsley, chopped
2 cups water

Yellow Rice

1 cup long-grain rice
2 cups water
1tsp salt
2 tsp tumeric
2 pieces stick cinnamon
4 pods cardamom

2 tbsp sugar
2 tbsp butter or margarine
1/2 cup raisins

Topping

1 tsp turmeric
1/2 tsp cinnamon powder
Pinch of salt
2 medium eggs

1 cup / 240 ml milk (including retained milk from soaked bread)
½ cup of flaked almonds or 4 bay leaves

Method

Pre-heat your oven to 400 F/200 C/Gas 6 and generously butter a large casserole pan with fairly high sides Soak the bread in the milk for about 20-30 minutes, until the milk is fully absorbed and the bread is really soft. Squeeze the bread to release some of the milk (don't throw away this milk).

Heat the oil in a large frying pan over medium heat. Add the onion and garlic and sweat until soft (about five minutes).

Add the ginger, curry powder, ground cumin, ground coriander and black pepper and fry for a couple of minutes Add water, apricots, sultanas, apple, lemon juice and lentils and cook for about 20 minutes until the lentils are soft.

Remove the pan from the heat and add the chopped almonds. Leave to cool a little. Stir in the soaked bread, parsley and black-eyed beans. Add this to the lentil mix and squash with your hand so the beans are partly, but not fully, mashed. This should make a moist but not watery mix.

Put into a baking ovenproof dish and smooth the top with a spoon.

For the Topping

Mix the egg with the retained milk from the soaked bread, adding more milk as necessary to make about 1 cup/240 ml. Mix in the turmeric, cinnamon and salt. Stir well. Pour this topping over the bean and lentil mix and put it in the oven. Top with flaked almonds or otherwise bay leaves.

Bake for 50-60 minutes or until the topping has set and is golden brown.

To make Yellow Rice

Wash 1 cup long-grain rice and add to 2 cups water, 1 tsp salt, 2 tsp tumeric, 2 pieces stick cinnamon and 4 pods cardamom and cook for about 20 minutes until soft.

Drain and rinse with cold water. Mix in 2 tbsp sugar, 2 tbsp butter or margarine and 1/2 cup raisins and cover and steam over medium heat for about 10 minutes.

Serving Options

Serve on top of yellow rice, accompanied by some of the accompaniments below: chutney (mango chutney works well) sliced tomatoes in a little vinegar with chopped chives, or spring onions on top sliced bananas green salad dried coconut diced cucumber and yoghurt

Bobotie is a very old South African dish with probable origins in Indonesia or Malaysia. The name derives from the Indonesian "bobotok," and the dish was likely adapted by Dutch traders and brought back to the region around Cape Town. Every South African cook has his or her own favourite version of this dish, some very simple, others quite elaborate. Bobotie is typically served with yellow rice and a side of mango chutney. This recipe below is a vegetarian version with lentils and black-eyed beans substituting traditionally used minced beef or lamb.

Marianne Bio

South African Marianne Du Toit has been living in Ireland for almost 20 years. In 2002 she undertook an epic adventure, traveling from Argentina to New York with only two horses for company. Her book titled Crying with Cockroaches is an account of her 21-month journey. Marianne lives in Dublin, does wedding and portrait photography and is involved with different animal welfare organisations

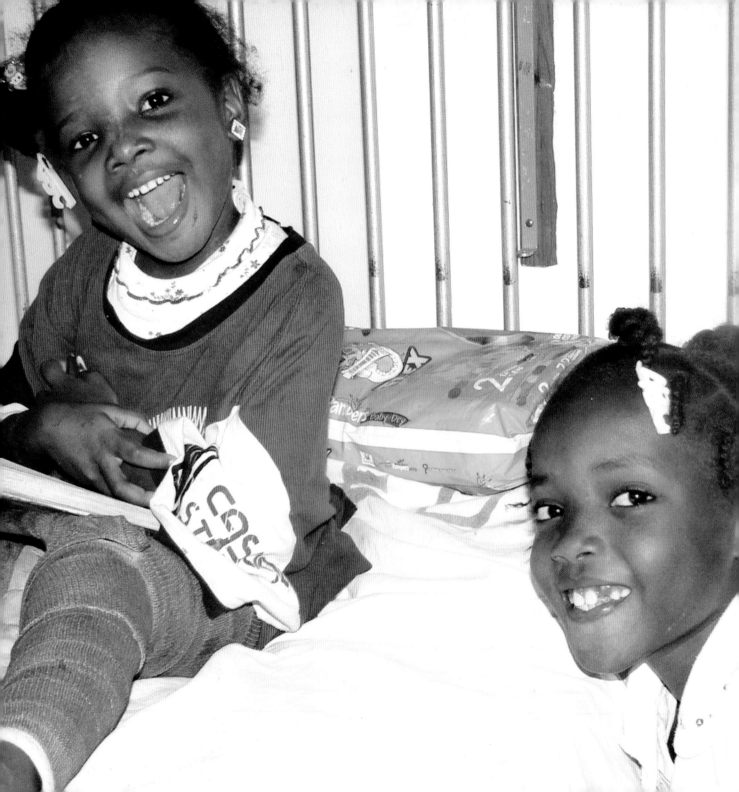

Sweet, Bread & Treat Recipe's

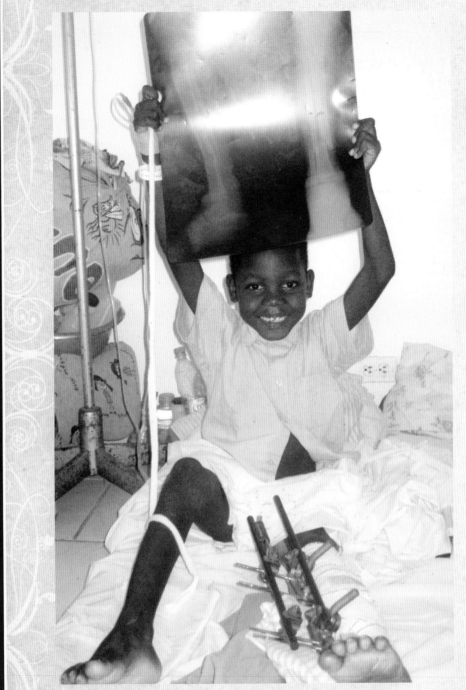

Blueberry Trifle

Ingredients (Serves 6-8)

6 eggs – separated
200g/7 oz caster sugar
1 vanilla pod
350g/12oz mascarpone cheese
275ml/1/2pt whipping cream, whipped
350g/12 oz blueberries
1 dsp water

juice of half lemon
1 hot-milk sponge cake
150 mls/1/4 pint sherry
Decoration
1 tbsp fresh blueberries
50g/2 oz flaked almonds-toasted

Method

Beat the egg yolks and 175g/6oz of the caster sugar in a heatproof bowl until pale and creamy. Add the vanilla pod, slit down one side and cook over a pan of simmering water for 5 –6 minutes, until the mixture thickens slightly and loses its eggy flavour. The best way to test if the mixture is ready is to taste it. Remove from heat, take out the vanilla pod and allow to cool. When almost cool, add the mascarpone cheese and cream alternately, a little at a time, mixing thoroughly after each addition.

Place the blueberries in a saucepan with the water, remaining sugar and the lemon juice. Heat gently for 1-2 minutes until the sugar has dissolved, then leave to cool.

Cut the cake into slices about 2.5cm/1 inch thick and arrange half in the bottom of a large serving dish. Pour over half the sherry and spoon over half the poached blueberries and half the mascarpone custard. Repeat all the layers, including the sherry, but reserve a little of the blueberry mixture for the top.

Decorate the top layer of mascarpone cream with the remaining poached blueberries, fresh blueberries and almonds. Alternatively serve the trifle in individual bowls or glasses.

Jenny Bristow One of Ireland's most celebrated local good food ambassador's, TV cooks and cookery writers.

Recipe for Disaster

ALL PROCEEDS IN AID OF IRISH ORTHOPAEDIC HAITI FUND

Rhubarb & Orange Cake with Flaked Almonds

Ingredients

400g (14oz) Irish rhubarb, trimmed
& cut into 2cm pieces
200g (7oz) golden caster sugar
150g (5.5oz) unsalted butter, softened
2 eggs, lightly beaten
75g (2.5oz) self-raising flour
0.5 tsp baking powder
100g (3.5oz) ground almonds, grated zest
and 2 tbsp juice of 1 small orange
25g (scant 1oz) flaked almonds

Method

Preheat the oven to 190C (375F/Gas mark 5) Grease and line the base of a 23cm (9") springform cake tin.
Place the rhubarb in a bowl and cover with 50g (2.5oz) of the sugar. Leave for 30 minutes while you prepare the rest of the cake.
With an electric whisk, beat together the remaining sugar and the butter in a bowl, then whisk in the eggs. Using a metal spoon, gently fold in the flour, baking powder and ground almonds, then stir in the orange zest and juice.
Stir the rhubarb and its sugary juices into the cake mixture and spoon into the prepared tin. Place on a baking tray, sprinkle over the flaked almonds and bake for 25 minutes. Reduce the temperature to 180C (350F/Gas mark 4) and cook for a further 20-25 minutes or until firm. Allow to cool in tin for 10 minutes.
Serve warm or cold with softly whipped cream or custard.

Cooking Time – 45 minutes

Makes 8-10 slices.

John Kearney
(Haiti February 2010)

88

Raspberry & Amaretti Crunch Cake

Ingredients (Serves 6-8)

175g soft butter
175g golden caster sugar
3 eggs
140g self-raising flour
85g ground almonds
140g Amaretti biscuits – roughly broken
250g punnet fresh raspberries (plus some extra for serving)
icing sugar to serve

Method

Preheat oven to 170°C.
Line the base and sides of a loose-based 20cm round cake tin
with parchment paper.
Place the butter, caster sugar, eggs flour and ground almonds into a bowl and beat
with an eletric whisk until well blended.
Roughly break up the amaretti biscuits.
Spread half the cake mixture in the lined tin. Scatter over half of the biscuits, then
half of the raspberries. Very lightly press these into the cake mixture.
Evenly spread the remaining cake mixture on top.
Scatter the remaining amaretti biscuits and the remaining half of the raspberries
over the cake mixture and lightly press into the cake mixture.
Bake for 55 – 65 minutes, until a skewer inserted into the centre comes out clean.
Allow to cool for 15 minutes in the tin. Then run a knife around the edge and turn
out onto a wire rack. Serve with fresh raspberries and softly whipped cream.

*In cooks Academy cookery school, this really tasty dessert features on our Easy
Entertaining course. We love it because it tastes so good, includes luxurious
ingredients such as fresh raspberries, amaretti biscuits and ground almonds and is
so easy to make. Enjoy.*

Cooks Academy founded in may 2005 by Vanessa and Tim Greenwood.

Recipe for Disaster

ALL PROCEEDS IN AID OF IRISH ORTHOPAEDIC HAITI FUND

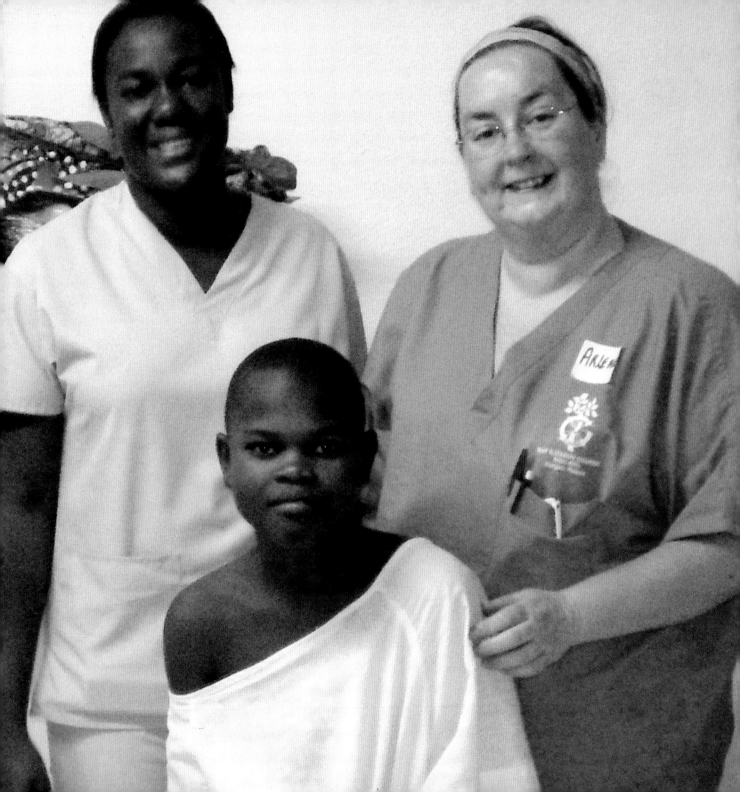

Chocolate Lover's Ice Cream

Ingredients

Egg custard
3 large eggs
75g (3 oz) caster sugar
450 ml (3/4) pint milk

350 g (12oz) white chocolate
300ml (½ pint) double cream, whipped
25g (1 oz) Meringues, roughly broken
100g (4oz) plain Chocolate

Decoration: 50g (2 oz) white chocolate

Method

Whisk the eggs and sugar together.
Warm the milk and pour onto the egg mixture whisking as you add it.
Return mixture to the saucepan and heat slowly until mixture starts to thicken, set to one side.

Melt half the white chocolate (6 oz) and stir into the custard.
Fold in the whipped cream. Put into freezer bowl (large enough to hold 1.5 litres or 3 pints) and freeze until mushy (2-3) hours.

While this is freezing, finely chop remaining white and plain chocolate and add to broken meringues.
Make chocolate leaves to decorate. Thoroughly wash and dry real holly or rose leaves. Melt chocolate and coat the underside of leaves, leave to set, then, gently peel leaf away from chocolate.

Remove ice cream from freezer and beat again to break up ice crystals. Stir in chocolate and meringue mixture. Return to freezer and freeze overnight. Ice cream can also be frozen in silicone bun cases for individual servings.
To serve: Plunge bowl in hot water for few seconds and turn onto serving dish. Decorate with chocolate leaves and serve in small slices. Silicone bun cases can be plunged into hot water for a few seconds and then turned out, decorated and served in individual dishes.

This is a very rich ice cream, ideal for a special occasion.
Mixed berries such as raspberries, cranberries and blueberries are the ideal accompaniment.

Arlene North Clinical Nurse Specialist, (Haiti February 2010)

Recipe for Disaster

ALL PROCEEDS IN AID OF IRISH ORTHOPAEDIC HAITI FUND

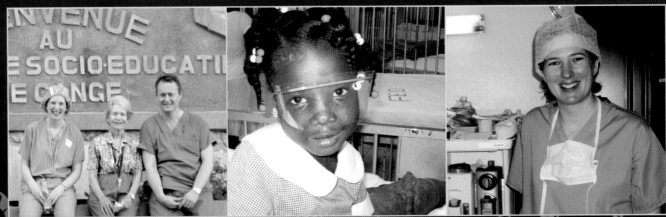

Pear and Almond Tart

Ingredients

6oz icing sugar
2oz plain flour
4oz ground almonds
5 egg whites
6oz butter, melted
2 ripe pears, peeled and cut into slices about a half centimetre thick
1oz flaked almonds

Method

Preheat the oven to 200C/400F/Gas 6.
Lightly grease the edges of a 9 inch tart tin with a removable base.
Sieve the icing sugar and flour into a clean bowl and stir in the ground almonds.
In another bowl whisk the egg whites for about 40 seconds until just frothy.
Add the egg whites and melted butter to the bowl containing the dry ingredients.
Mix all together until smooth and pour the mixture into the greased tart tin.
Arrange the pear slices on the top of the mixture and sprinkle the flaked almonds on top of the pears.
Put the tin in the oven and bake for 15 minutes, then turn down the heat of the oven to 180C/350F/Gas 4 and cook for a further ten minutes or until firm to the touch and a pale golden colour. Remove the tin from the oven and allow sit for a few minutes before turning it out onto a wire rack.
Dust with icing sugar before serving.
Enjoy with ice cream and good company.

This is my favourite of my mother's famous tart recipes as, even with my limited culinary accomplishments (my father's side unfortunately), it never fails to impress.

Niamh Conlon Consultant Anaesthetist (Haiti February 2010)

SWEETS, BREAD & TREATS

Recipe for Disaster

ALL PROCEEDS IN AID OF IRISH ORTHOPAEDIC HAITI FUND

Cardamon, Plum and Fig Cake

The secret of this cake is to pack it so full of ripe plums – top and bottom- that it can be served either way up. Choose plums that are ripe but firm so they will hold their shape when cooked.

Ingredients

450g/1lb plums – halved and stoned
450g/1lb figs – quartered
zest of 1 lime
6-8 cardamon pods – roughly crushed
25g/1 oz Demerara sugar
4 eggs
175g/6oz caster sugar
250g/9oz self-raising flour- sieved
175g/6oz butter – softened
50g/2oz ground almonds
50g/2oz flaked almonds
2dsp runny honey
½ tsp vanilla extract
2-3 dsp milk – optional
Demerara sugar or icing sugar for dusting flavoured with cinnamon or mixed spice

Method

Place the plums and figs in a large bowl with the zest, cardamon and sugar and leave to infuse for 15 minutes.

Beat the eggs and sugar until the mixture is light and fluffy and forms soft peaks Add the flour and butter, mixing lightly. Finally, add the ground and flaked almonds, honey and vanilla extract and mix well. If the mixture is a little stiff, add a little milk.

Line a loose-bottomed cake tin (18-20cm/7-8 inches) with greaseproof paper. Remove the cardamon pods from the bowl and arrange a layer of plums and figs on the bottom of the cake tin. Pour the cake mixture over the fruit and smooth the surface with a spatula. Arrange the remaining fruit on top of the cake. Bake in the oven @ 180°C/ gas mark 4 for 45- 50 minutes until the cake is cooked, golden and firm. Remove the cake from the oven and sprinkle with a little Demerara or dust with icing sugar. Delicious served hot or cold, on its own or topped with yoghurt and honey.

Jenny Bristow One of Ireland's most celebrated local good food ambassador's, TV cooks and cookery writers.

Recipe for Disaster

ALL PROCEEDS IN AID OF IRISH ORTHOPAEDIC HAITI FUND

Pavlova

Ingredients
3 egg whites
6 oz caster sugar
pinch salt.

Method
Line a baking sheet with baking paper or use silicone sheet.
Whisk egg whites with pinch of salt until they form soft peaks.
Whisk in sugar a little at a time, whisking well after each addition
until smooth and glossy.
Spoon 3/4 of mixture into 8 inch round. Spoon rest of mixture around edge to
make a nest shape.
Bake in pre heated oven 140° C/275 °F, Gas mark 1 for 1 1/4 hours.
Allow to cool.

Lemon curd How to use up egg yolks from making a meringue.

Ingredients
3 oz cornflour
6oz caster sugar
3/4 pint water
rind and juice 3 lemons
3 egg yolks
1 oz butter

Method
Place cornflour and sugar in saucepan, gradually whisk in water, add lemon rind
and butter and bring to boil, continuously stirring until thick and transparent.
Remove from heat and stir in lemon juice. Beat in egg yolks.
Allow to cool and put into cooled Pavlova nest.

Whip 300 mls of cream. Put on top of lemon curd in Pavlova nest.
Sprinkle passion fruit seeds on top.
Enjoy.

Erica Flood Theatre CNMI (Haiti February 2010)

Recipe for Disaster

ALL PROCEEDS IN AID OF IRISH ORTHOPAEDIC HAITI FUND

Chocolate Biscuit Cake

Ingredients

225g (8 oz) roughly broken rich tea or Marie biscuits
75g (3 oz) butter
2 tbsp golden syrup
1 tbsp cocoa
1 tsp vanilla essence (orange or coffee can be used either)
230g milk chocolate

Method

1 lb loaf tin lined with silicone liner.
Grate almost half the chocolate onto the base of the tin. (the hot biscuit mix will melt this chocolate when added)

Put golden syrup, butter and cocoa in a heavy base saucepan.
Melt over a low heat stirring all the time. When melted bring to rolling boil and immediately remove from heat. Stir in flavouring of choice.
Add biscuits ensuring all are coated in mixture.
Turn into prepared tin and compress down and smooth on top.
Leave to cool slightly.
Melt remaining chocolate in a bowl over a pot of boiling water.
Pour over biscuit cake and leave to set in refrigerator overnight.
Slice thickly and enjoy.

For when I NEED to indulge myself
David Moore Orthopaedic Surgeon, Orthopaedic team Haiti February 2010

Recipe *for* Disaster

ALL PROCEEDS IN AID OF IRISH ORTHOPAEDIC HAITI FUND

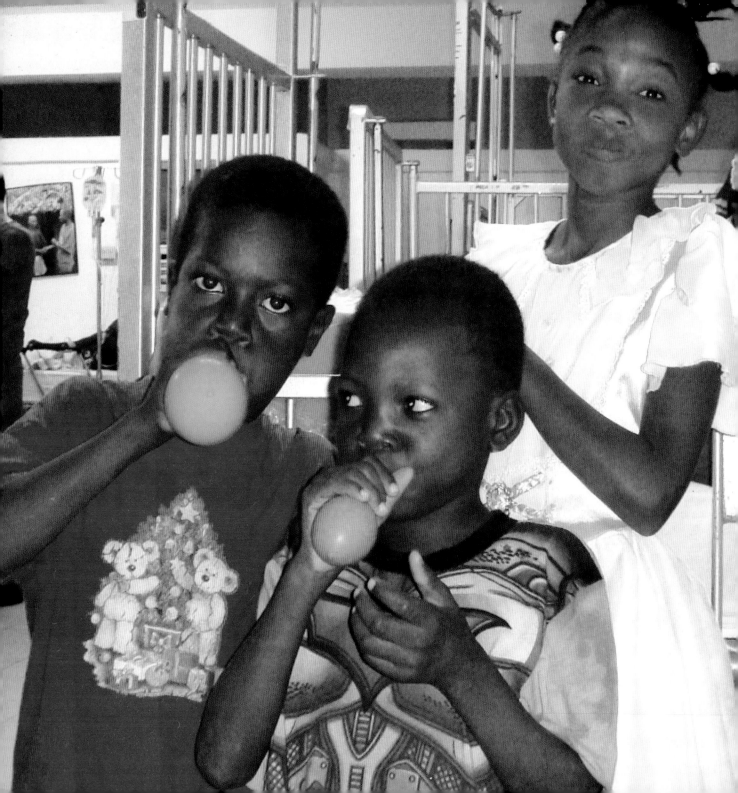

Balloons

Ingredients
140g/5oz/ 1 scant cup of flour
2tsp caster sugar
pinch of salt
milk
extra caster sugar

Method
Put flour, sugar and baking powder into a bowl and mix well.
Make a well in the middle and pour in approximately 11/2 cups of milk.
Stir the flour gradually beating out the lumps as you go, add more milk until you get a soft "dropping" consistency.
Heat the oil, or better still, beef dripping to 190°C/385°F. Drop in spoonfuls of the batter to swell up and brown.
Remove and drain.
Place on absorbent paper with caster sugar and roll immediately.

Myrtle Allen Ballymaloe House

Recipe for Disaster

ALL PROCEEDS IN AID OF IRISH ORTHOPAEDIC HAITI FUND

Little Pecan Puffs

Ingredients Makes 48
110g/4oz pecan nuts
110g/4oz/1stick butter – softened
50g/2oz/1/4 cup caster sugar
1 tsp vanilla extract
100g/4oz/1cup plain flour
25g/1oz/1/4 cup icing sugar sifted onto shallow bowl or plate

Method
Preheat the oven to 150°C/300°F/Gas mark 2.
Place the pecan nuts in a food processor and grind until quite fine.
In a bowl cream the butter, then add the sugar and vanilla and beat until light and fluffy.
Add the ground pecan nuts and flour and bring together to form a dough. Roll into small marble size balls of dough between the palms of your hands, then flatten slightly using the palm of your hand and place on baking tray.
Bake for 40 minutes.
Allow to cool for 2 minutes, then carefully remove from the tray, and while they are still hot roll them in the sifted icing sugar. Cool on a wire rack, and when cooled sift with icing sugar again.

Tip: These will keep for 5 – 6 days very well or they can be frozen.

Rachel Allen Ballymaloe Cookery School Irish Celebrity chef, known most widely for her work on television and as a writer

Recipe *for* Disaster

ALL PROCEEDS IN AID OF IRISH ORTHOPAEDIC HAITI FUND

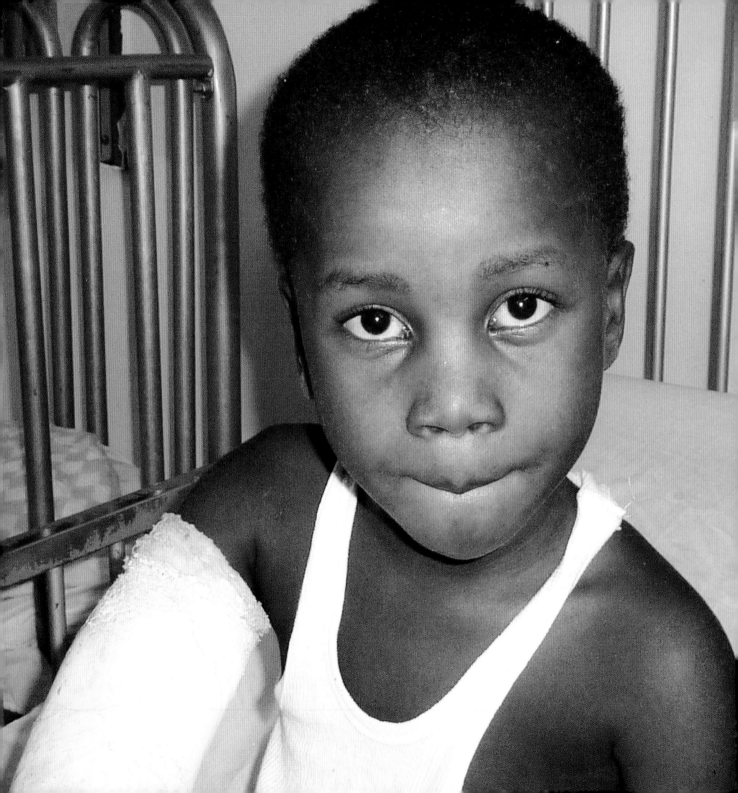

Almond Slices

Ingredients

Pastry
8oz plain flour
1 pinch of salt
4 oz margarine
1 egg yolk
1 tablespoon water

Apricot jam
4oz caster sugar
4oz icing sugar
4 oz ground almonds
2oz semolina or farola
1 whole egg
1 egg white
1 tsp almond essence
4oz split almonds or chopped almonds

Method
Preheat oven to 200°C/400°F/Gas mark 6.
Make pastry, roll out and put in tin.
Spread thinly with jam.
For topping mix all dry ingredients. Stir in beaten eggs(1 egg & 1 egg white) and essence.
Top pastry with this mixture and decorate with almonds.
Bake near top of oven for 25-30 minutes.

This is a recipe for my Mam's Famous Almond slices. Well famous in our house anyway, they were lovely.

Brendan Gleeson Irish actor his best known films include *Braveheart, Gangs of New York, In Bruges, 28 Days Later,* the *Harry Potter Films,* and the role of Michael Collins in *The Treaty*. He won an Emmy Award in 2009 for his protrayal of Winston Churchill in *Into the Storm*

Recipe for Disaster

ALL PROCEEDS IN AID OF IRISH ORTHOPAEDIC HAITI FUND

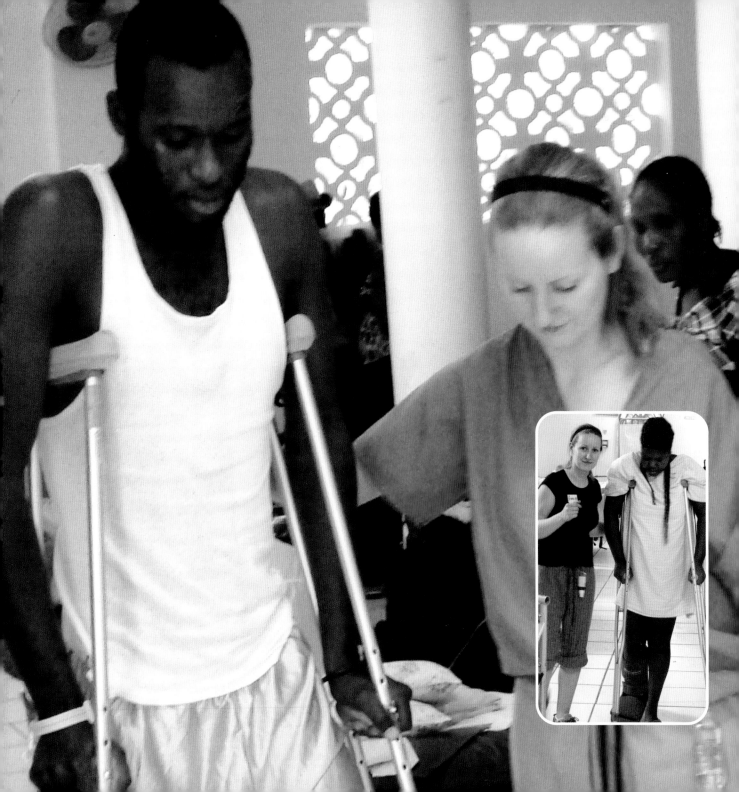

Chocolate Almond Truffles

Ingredients
200 mg milk chocolate
100ml double cream
15g unsalted butter
Chopped almonds
Almond extract

Method
Break chocolate into small pieces in a bowl.
Put cream and butter into a saucepan & slowly bring to the boil. Once boiling immediately pour over the chocolate and stir with a wooden spoon until mixture is smooth & all the chocolate has melted.
Stir in a few drops of almond.
Cover & allow to cool at room temperature for 30mins and then chill in the fridge for 2 hours.
Using a small spoon scoop out bite-sized pieces – dust your hands very lightly with cocoa powder and roll into balls.
Immediately roll each ball in the chopped almonds & place into foil cases.
Chill in the fridge – they will keep for 10 days. Best served from chilled as go very soft at room temperature! Enjoy!!

This recipe was only recently passed onto me but I have made great use of it already. They are easy to make – albeit a bit messy at first! So delicious and look very impressive too!

Anna Magnier Chartered Physiotherapist (Haiti February 2010)

Recipe for Disaster

...ALL PROCEEDS IN AID OF IRISH ORTHOPAEDIC HAITI FUND

Carrot Kheer

Ingredients

Carrots 1 Cup
Custard Powder (vanilla Flavour) 1 tsp
Ground Carrots 1/2 Cup
Roasted Nuts 2 tbsp
Sugar 1 Cup
Whole Milk 3-4 Cup

Method

Take a heavy pan and bring milk to boil. Add the grated and ground carrot to the milk and mix. Let the carrots cook well and soft. Better not use any water.
 Add more milk if the mixture is too thick. It should be of thin consistency at this point. Add sugar (according to your sweet tooth). Add cardamon powder.
Check the taste. Mix custard powder in warm milk and add to the cooking kheer on slow flame. Add little by little, checking the consistency.
It should be of kheer (thickened consistency) after a boil.
Turn off the heat and add roasted nuts.
It tastes great both warm and refrigerate cool.

Sudha Yerukonda Theatre Nurse (Haiti February 2010)

Recipe *for* Disaster

ALL PROCEEDS IN AID OF IRISH ORTHOPAEDIC HAITI FUND

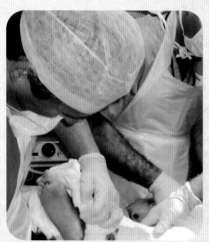

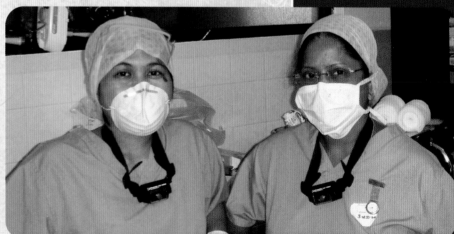

Brown Bread

Ingredients

6oz of Porridge Oats
8oz extra coarse wholemeal flour
125ml tub of Bio Yoghurt
1 Egg
1 tsp baking powder
1 tsp bread soda
¼ tsp salt
1 tsp golden granulated sugar
1 pint of milk
Handful of wheat germ
Handful of mixed seeds
Sesame seeds

Method

Heat oven to 160° C.
Grease a 2lb loaf tin.
Mix all dry ingredients together in a bowl.
Mix egg, yoghurt together in a measuring jug
and add enough milk to make to 1 pint.
Add this to the dry ingredients and mix well.
Turn the mixture into a tin.
Make a longways incision in the mixture.
Sprinkle sesame seeds on top
Bake for 50-60 minutes

*"I love this brown bread in the mornings with coarse cut marmala   after my
bowl of porridge. I sometimes have it for lunch also with chicker   n top"*

Ronan Collins Irish Radio and Television Personality

SWEETS, BREAD & TREATS

Recipe for Disaster

ALL PROCEEDS IN AID OF IRISH ORTHOPAEDIC HAITI FUND

Savoury Muffins

Ingredients

360g self-raising flour
1 tsp sugar
Pinch of salt
100ml oil
2eggs
300ml buttermilk
100gm meat
80gm cheese
5 scallions

Method

Sieve flour, sugar, and salt into large bowl.
Whisk oil eggs and buttermilk and fold into flour mix with the flavourings.
Fill into muffin cases or smaller if desired.
Bake in hot oven 180°c gas 5 20- 30 minutes depending on size

I usually just use the regular bun tin size and this makes 24.

This is one of my favourite recipes because it is quick and easy to make. If you have unexpected guests you can have these in and out of the oven before the kettle is boiled!

Freda Fleming former proprietor of Fleming's coffee shop, Monaghan, chef and now freelance cookery teacher.

Recipe for Disaster

ALL PROCEEDS IN AID OF IRISH ORTHOPAEDIC HAITI FUND

Recipe for Disaster

ALL PROCEEDS IN AID OF IRISH ORTHOPAEDIC HAITI FUND

Baked Raspberry and White Chocolate Cheesecake

Ingredients

300g cream cheese
120g caster sugar
200g mascarpone cheese
2 Free range eggs
170g raspberries(fresh or frozen)
80g white chocolate
1/2 packet of digestive biscuits
30g butter

Method

Try to use a baking or quiche tin around 8 inches in diameter
Grease your tin before making your biscuit base
Blend digestives in a food processor. Add melted butter
Refrigerate until cheese mix is ready
In a mixing bowl beat your cream cheese, mascarpone, eggs and sugar till
nice and fluffy.
Add your white chocolate and raspberries and gently fold into the mixture don't
over do it. Remember your cheesecake is not supposed to change colour.
Pour your mix over your digestives an bake for 30mins at 220°c
Fan assisted ovens may take a little less time
Refrigerate for two hours before serving

Kevin Ahern Chef Proprietor Sage Restaurant Midleton, Co. Cork

Christophe's Chocolate and Walnut Brownie

Ingredients

300g white sugar
4 eggs
5 oz self raising flour

200 melted chocolate
250g melted butter
150g chopped walnuts

Method
Preheat oven to 180°C
Line 10' baking tin approx 1 inch deep with butter greaseproof paper.
Beat eggs and sugar until white and creamy in a mixer.
Turn down mixer to a low-speed and spoon in flour.
Pour in melted chocolate.
Pour in melted butter.
Add chopped walnuts.
Pour mixture into pre-lined baking tin.
Cook for 40-50 minutes.
Serve warm with freshly whipped cream.

Christophe's Restaurant, Smithfield, Dublin 7

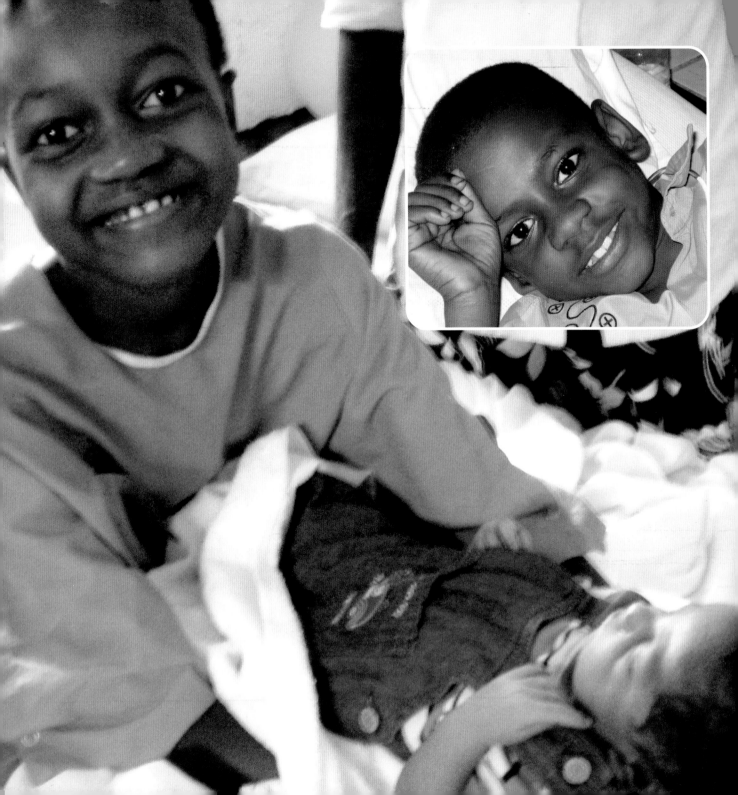

Cupcakes

Ingredients

125g/4 oz Odlums self-raising flour
125g/4 oz caster sugar
125g/4oz Butter or margarine – at
room temperature

2 eggs – at room temperature
few drops of vanilla essence
Preparation time 10 minutes
Baking time 15 minutes

Method

Ensure oven is fully pre-heated to 180°C/350°F/Gas mark 4. Line cup cake tin with
baking cases.
Beat the butter and sugar together until light and fluffy. Gradually beat in the eggs
and the vanilla essence. If the mixture starts to curdle, add a little of the flour.
Gently stir in remaining flour with a spoon. Place spoonfuls of the mixture into the
baking cases and bake for 15 – 20 minutes until firm to the touch
Remove from the oven and leave on a wire tray to cool

For Toppings

Hazelnut chocolate spread
Shamrock ready to roll icing
CPAC instant royal Icing
Buttercream: Beat 75g/3 oz of butter or margarine until soft. Add 175g/6oz of
sieved icing sugar, 1 tbsp of boiling water and a few drops of vanilla essence.
Beat until smooth and pale in colour.
Glace icing: Sieve 225g/8oz icing sugar into a bowl, beat in 2-3 tbsp of water
(adding 1 spoon at a time!) until a thick smooth icing is achieved

Catherine Leyden TV3 Cook

Recipe for Disaster

ALL PROCEEDS IN AID OF IRISH ORTHOPAEDIC HAITI FUND

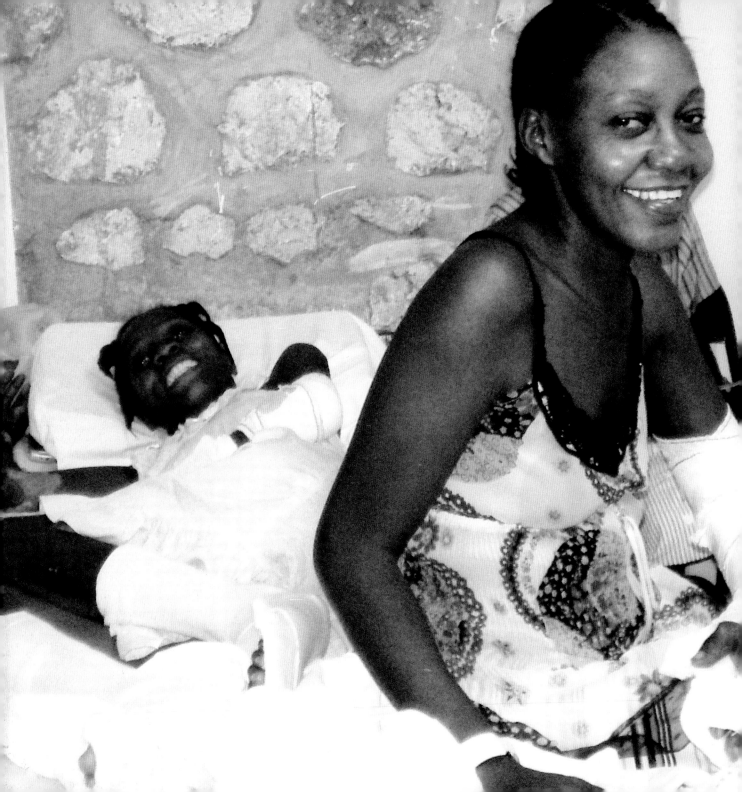

Chilli Jam

Ingredients

1/2 cup vegetable oil
1 red onion
1 red pepper
3 red chilli
4 green chilli
2 bullet chilli
5 cloves garlic
1 knob of ginger
1/4 cup fish sauce
10 tomatoes

Method

De-seed the chilli and the peppers.
Dice all ingredients to roughly the size of the top of your baby finger.
In a wide based pot heat the oil making sure the oil is very hot, carefully add the diced veg. (Not the tomatoes.) Try not to splatter yourself [it will hurt]
Now turn your heat to medium cook the veg for 20mins stirring occasionally.
Now add your tomatoes and sugar simmer for a further 10 minutes.
Add fish sauce.
Simmer for a further 5 minutes.
Finish.
Allow jam to cool before you refrigerate.

This jam is great with a lot of things. I use it with flash fried calamari, but it can be used as a salsa or base for pizza or just on its own for a dip. It's a great topping for burgers too.

Kevin Aherne Chef Proprietor Sage Restaurant, Midleton, Co Cork

Summer Sangria

Ingredients

1 litre of red wine (Merlot is a good choice)
1 lime
1 lemon
1 orange
1 shot of brandy
1 can of ginger-ale
1 litre of soda water
A handful of fresh mint
1 cinnamon stick
Fresh strawberries

Method

Slice limes, lemons, oranges and strawberries 1/2 an inch thick.
Once this is done it really is just a case of putting everything
together and refrigerating. Just make sure its made 2-3 hours in advance for the
flavours to fuse together.

Kevin Aherne Chef Proprietor Sage Restaurant, Midleton, Co Cork

Recipe for Disaster

ALL PROCEEDS IN AID OF IRISH ORTHOPAEDIC HAITI FUND

Recipe for Disaster

ALL PROCEEDS IN AID OF IRISH ORTHOPAEDIC HAITI FUND

INDEX

Haitian Recipes

Starter Recipes

Main Courses

Sweet, Bread and Treat Recipes

INDEX

Recipe *for* Disaster

ALL PROCEEDS IN AID OF IRISH ORTHOPAEDIC HAITI FUND

Recipe *for* Disaster
ALL PROCEEDS IN AID OF IRISH ORTHOPAEDIC HAITI FUND

OVEN TEMPERATURES

DEGREES FAHRENHEIT	DEGREES CENTIGRADE	GAS MARK
220	100	LOW
225	110	1/4
250	120	1/2
275	140	1
300	150	2
325	160	3
350	170	4
375	180	5
400	190	6
425	200	7
450	230	8
475	240	9

MEASURING SPOONS

TSP	Teaspoon	5 Millilitres
DSP	Dessertspoon	10 Millilitres
TBSP	Tablespoon	15 Millilitres

Pounds & Ounces	Grams
1/2 oz	14g
1oz	28g
2oz	56g
3oz	85g
4oz	113g
5oz	142g
6oz	170g
8oz	227g
10oz	283g
12oz	340g
14oz	397g
16oz / 1lb	454g

Notes